GREAT WESTERN RAILWAY GALLERY

A PICTORIAL JOURNEY THROUGH TIME

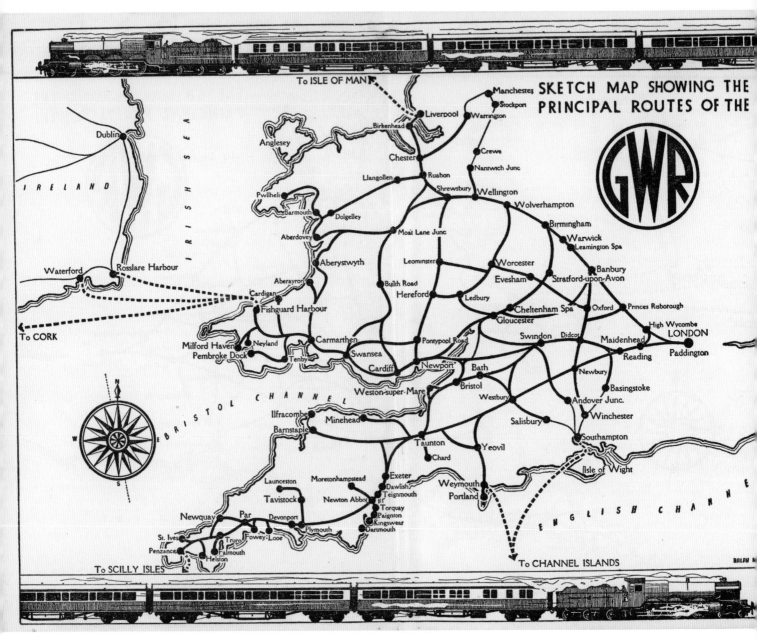

A map published in 1936 showing principal routes of the Great Western Railway.

Front Cover: A down service passes Bleadon and Uphill station in the early 1900s hauled by a pair of Gooch designed 4-2-2s nos 3029 *White Horse* and 3011 *Greyhound*. They were built as 2-2-2s but rebuilt as 4-2-2s in October 1894 and November 1891 respectively.

Back cover top left: *Great Western*

Back cover top right: Cheltenham Flyer

Back cover centre: *The Great Bear*

Back cover centre inset: The Great Western Railway Coat- of- Arms incorporating the shields, crests and mottoes of London (left) 'Lord Guide Us', and Bristol (right).'Power and Energy'.

Back cover bottom: Cornish Riviera Express

GREAT WESTERN RAILWAY GALLERY

A PICTORIAL JOURNEY THROUGH TIME

LAURENCE WATERS

PEN & SWORD
TRANSPORT

AN IMPRINT OF PEN & SWORD BOOKS LTD.
YORKSHIRE – PHILADELPHIA

First published in Great Britain in 2018 by
Pen and Sword Transport
An imprint of
Pen & Sword Books Ltd
Yorkshire - Philadelphia

ISBN 978 1 52670 703 1

A CIP catalogue record for this book is available from the British Library.

Typeset by Aura Technology and Software Services, India
Printed and bound in India by Replika Press Pvt. Ltd.

Pen & Sword Books Ltd incorporates the Imprints of Pen & Sword Books Archaeology, Atlas, Aviation, Battleground, Discovery, Family History, History, Maritime, Military, Naval, Politics, Railways, Select, Transport, True Crime, Fiction, Frontline Books, Leo Cooper, Praetorian Press, Seaforth Publishing, Wharncliffe and White Owl.

For a complete list of Pen & Sword titles please contact

PEN & SWORD BOOKS LIMITED
47 Church Street, Barnsley, South Yorkshire, S70 2AS, England
E-mail: enquiries@pen-and-sword.co.uk
Website: www.pen-and-sword.co.uk

or

PEN AND SWORD BOOKS
1950 Lawrence Rd, Havertown, PA 19083, USA
E-mail: Uspen-and-sword@casematepublishers.com
Website: www.penandswordbooks.com

CONTENTS

FOREWORD

The subject of the Great Western Railway must be amongst the most widely published of railway focused books of all time, and yet another book might be expected to be wearing out what's new that can be said or shown. As Chairman and Collection Manager of the Great Western Trust, whose archive has been so skilfully harvested by Laurence Waters for this publication, I can assure readers that the archive is such a rich and vast seam of previously unpublished material, that it is our objective to work with Pen & Sword to make this book the first of a series solely based on our unique collection. A very significant responsibility within our Charitable purposes is the education and enjoyment of everyone who seeks to know more about the GWR, its Constituent, Absorbed and Joint Companies and indeed of the nationalised British Railways Western Region. This book, and we hope its future series companions, will continue that activity of the Trust, and in so doing widen the community of GWR enthusiasts beyond those focused on its locomotives and rolling stock. In its core contents the Trust Archive is more representative of transport and social history, as reflected in one long lasting and successful railway company. Do enjoy this book.

Peter Rance, Chairman, Great Western Trust (Regd Charity 289008)

ACKNOWLEDGEMENTS

Within the pages I have tried to illustrate the many facets that made up the Great Western Railway. Certainly during the period from the early 1900s and up until nationalisation, the Great Western had an exceptional publicity department and I have included many examples of its work within these pages. All of the material used in the book is from the superb 'Great Western Trust' collection at Didcot Railway Centre, and I would like to thank the Trustees for allowing me access to this material. However, the constraints of the book have meant that some areas of the system have probably not had the coverage that they deserve; for this I apologise. All images used in the book are pre-1947.

I would also like to thank the following for their help: William Turner for patiently restoring a number of the images; Peter Simmons for his remarks and advice regarding the content; Graham Carpenter for his knowledge of Great Western rolling stock; and to the Trust's Wednesday photo team for their constant support.

In producing this book, I have consulted the following publications.
Burdett Wilson, Roger, *Go Great Western*
Macdermot, E.T., *History of the Great Western Railway*
Lyons/Mountford, *GWR Engine Sheds*, Vols 1 and 2
RCTS *The Locomotives of the Great Western Railway*
Clinker's Register f Closed Passenger Stations
Peto's Registers of Great Western Locomotives

Laurence Waters Oxford 2018.

INTRODUCTION

The Great Western Railway was a wonderful railway, the only major railway company in this country to retain its identity from its inception in 1835 right up until the nationalisation of the Railways on 1 January 1948. The Company can trace its origins back even earlier, to August 1832 when four Bristol businessmen, George Jones, John Harford, Thomas Guppy and

Arguably Britain's greatest railway engineer, Isambard Kingdom Brunel. Born at Portsea, Portsmouth on 9 April 1806, Chief Engineer to the Great Western Railway 1833-1859, died London 15 September 1859.

William Tothill held an informal meeting with the idea of resurrecting an earlier but unsuccessful idea of a railway between Bristol and London. After a number of meetings, in January 1833 the committee, which had now expanded to 15 members, agreed to fund a preliminary survey and to appoint an engineer, and on 7 March 1833 the committee made what was arguably its most important decision by appointing the 27-year-old engineer Isambard Kingdom Brunel. Brunel was the son of the French civil engineer Marc Isambard Brunel and Sophia Kingdom and was born in Portsmouth on 9 April 1806. In April 1826 at the age of just 20, he took over the position as an assistant engineer on the Thames Tunnel working under his father, who was the chief engineer of the project.

Once appointed by the Bristol and London committee, Brunel, together with William Turner, a land surveyor, undertook a rather rapid survey of the proposed route. This was completed by the middle of June. Brunel suggested that route should run via Chippenham, Swindon, across the Vale of the White Horse and along the Thames Valley, with the cost of construction estimated to be around £2,800,000. His report confirmed the viability of the project and was accepted by the board at a meeting at Bristol on 30 July 1833 where the following resolution was passed:

'A company should be formed for the establishment of railway communications between Bristol and London, and for that purpose of a body of directors for Bristol be appointed, who, in conjunction with a similar body to be appointed in London, shall constitute a general board of management for securing subscriptions and obtaining an Act of Parliament for effecting the same object'.

On 19 August 1833, the newly formed Bristol & London Committee adopted the name 'Great Western Railway'. After a number of early setbacks, mainly due to lack of funds, the bill received its Royal Assent on 31 August 1835 and the Great Western Railway was born.

Interestingly, the bill went through parliament without any mention of the gauge of the new railway. Was it just an oversight, or did Brunel ask the Company to exclude this important information, for its omission allowed Brunel to consider the track gauge of the new railway? He had always advocated that a wide gauge would allow high speeds together with exceptional stability. It would also allow the boilers of locomotive to be placed within the frames rather than on top, again aiding stability. In a report to the company on 15 September 1835, Brunel proposed a track gauge of between 6ft 10in and 7ft 0in. The gauge adopted was 7ft 0in, later 7ft 0¼in, to ease clearance.

Even for someone as vain as Brunel this must have been a dream job. Soon after the construction had started he proclaimed:

'The railway is now in progress. I am thus engineer to the finest work in England. A handsome salary, on excellent terms with my directors and all going smoothly'.

On 13 August 1837, 21-year old Daniel Gooch was appointed as the first 'Superintendent of Locomotive Engines'. Gooch soon became an important man; with the poor reliability of many of the early locomotives, it was Gooch together with his small team of engineers that kept these locomotives in action, and services running during the early days of the railway.

The first 24 mile section of the Great Western Railway was opened between Paddington and Maidenhead on 4 June 1838 with eight passenger services each weekday and six on Sundays. It was recorded that at the end of the first week of operation some 10,360 passengers were carried with receipts of £1,552. Gradually, services were extended westwards, reaching Twyford in July 1839 and Reading in March 1840, by which time annual passenger numbers had risen to over a million. The line between Reading and Wootton Bassett was opened in stages this section being completed on 17 December 1840. The Western section between Bristol and Bath was opened on 31 August 1840. A landmark was reached on 30 June 1841 when services were extended through to Bristol. The delay in opening this last stretch of line between Bath and Chippenham was due to the construction of the Box Tunnel. Work began on the tunnel in September 1836; excavating from each end, it took up to 1,000 men and 100 horses some five years to remove the 247,000 tons of spoil. On 30 June 1841, the 3,212 yard tunnel was opened for use.

The new railway was not without problems. Sonning Cutting became the scene of the first major accident when, on the morning of Christmas Eve 1841, the 4.30am down goods service hauled by the 2-4-0 Leo class *Hecla* ran into a landslip which had occurred near the centre of the cutting. The train that comprised two third class carriages and 18 goods wagons was derailed. Unfortunately the two third class vehicles (open wagons) contained 38 passengers with many being crushed by the heavy goods vehicles. 18 passengers were killed and 17 seriously injured. The crash was made worse as at this time rail vehicles were not fitted with spring buffers. The report on the accident led to the Gladstone's act of 1844 which looked into the way third class passengers were carried.

Services were extended to Exeter via Bristol on 1 May 1844, and from Exeter to Plymouth in May 1848. The opening of the Royal Albert Bridge at Saltash in May 1859 saw services extended through to Penzance.

On 18 June 1850, the South Wales Railway opened between Swansea and Chepstow, and on 19 September 1851, the Great Western opened its own line from Gloucester to a temporary station called

Not a locomotive in sight but plenty of broad gauge coaches and wagons, some carrying B&ER logos, are seen here in this early shot of the Bristol and Exeter station at Plymouth Millbay. The station was closed to passenger services on 23 April 1941, the yard remained open for goods until 20 June 1966. The large building in the background is the Duke of Cornwall hotel, opened in 1865 and still in business today.

Chepstow East. Standing between the two lines was the River Wye; the connection was made on 19 July 1852 with the opening of Brunel's new tubular suspension bridge that crossed the river at Chepstow. This now allowed through services to operate between Paddington and South Wales, via Swindon, and Gloucester. The South Wales main line was gradually extended westward, and in April 1856, through services were inaugurated between Paddington and New Milford (Leyland), which for a number of years was the terminus of the line. Interestingly, it was not until August 1906 that the line reached Fishguard Harbour, via a new line from Clarbeston Junction to Letterston Junction.

The Midlands were eventually served by the opening of the Oxford Railway between Didcot and Oxford in June 1844. The line being extended to Banbury in October 1850, to Birmingham in October 1852, and to Wolverhampton in November 1854.

Brunel's broad gauge was a wonderful railway, but with every other railway company using the 4ft 8½ inches (narrow) gauge, the broad gauge became an anachronism, and on 25 June 1845, the government set up the Gauge Commission to look at the uniformity of gauge in this country. After a lot of deliberation, on 18 August 1846 the Gauge Act, as it became known, was given Royal Ascent. The Act forbade the future construction of any railway for the conveyance of passengers on any gauge other than 4ft 8½in. in Great Britain and 5ft 3in in Ireland. Interestingly it still allowed the construction of broad gauge lines, and despite opposition, Acts were obtained for the construction of broad gauge lines in the Midlands, South Wales and Devon and Cornwall. On 1 September 1854, the Great Western took over the narrow gauge Shrewsbury and Chester and Shrewsbury and Birmingham Railway, and in 1855,

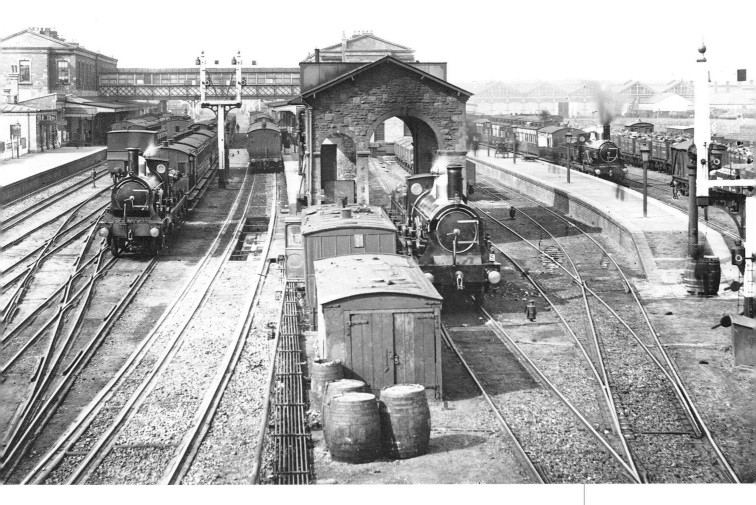

the first narrow gauge locomotives were built at Swindon. The writing was on the wall as in 1869, broad gauge working was withdrawn north of Oxford and three years later the broad gauge was removed from the South Wales main line and all connecting branches, and during the same year broad gauge services were removed between Oxford and Didcot. The decline of the broad gauge continued,and at their meeting on 19 March 1891, the Great Western Board agreed that the final conversion of the remaining broad gauge lines to narrow gauge should take place in May 1892. The final conversion work took place over the weekend of 21 & 22 May when some 4,700 men converted 177 miles of track from broad to standard gauge in just 31 hours. At Swindon, some 15 miles of sidings had previously been laid to accommodate the 196 locomotives,347 carriages and 3,544 goods wagons made redundant by the removal of the Broad Gauge.

For many years, the GWR was rather jokingly referred to as the 'great way round' and not without due cause. The South West was reached via Bristol; Birmingham and Wolverhampton were reached via Oxford; and services to South Wales ran via Gloucester. This was addressed with the opening to passenger services of the 8 mile long Severn Tunnel Railway from Pilning Junction to Severn Tunnel Junction, on 1 December 1886; this now allowed through services to South Wales run via Bristol instead of Gloucester. The Severn Tunnel is a superb feat of engineering. It is 4 miles 624 yards in length and took 14 years to build. On 5 September 1885, a special train carrying Sir Daniel and Lady Gooch ran through the tunnel from Severn Tunnel Junction to a siding on the Gloucestershire side as the track had not yet been laid through to Pilning. The first train to run through the tunnel on the newly completed Severn Tunnel Railway was an experimental

Swindon Junction station in the early 1890s, with mixed gauge tracks still in evidence on the main line. The Swindon to Gloucester line on the right was converted from broad to standard gauge in May 1872. All three locomotives in view are standard gauge 2-4-0s.

A view of the eastern portal of the Severn Tunnel taken in around 1885 and some time prior to its official opening to passenger traffic on 1 December 1886.

coal train from Aberdare to Southampton on 9 January 1886. After some further work, mainly on the pumping station at Sudbrook, it was opened for goods traffic on 1 September 1886, but it was not until 1 December of the same year that it was finally opened for passenger traffic. The cost of the new line and tunnel was recorded as £1,806,248. The Great Western were constantly improving the system to increase the line capacity and, by 1890, they had installed four tracks between Paddington and Didcot, a task that included widening Brunel's bridge over the Thames at Maidenhead. During the same period, the single line sections on the main line through Devon and Cornwall were gradually doubled.

Excursion traffic formed an important part of Great Western railway operations. Excursions were a good way of introducing the general public to rail travel, which in turn produced extra revenue. Another aspect of the excursion was the extra trade that the influx of 'excursionists' brought to the local economy. Local tradesmen certainly welcomed the arrival of the excursion trains. It is probably true to say that the growth of excursion trains triggered the growth in many towns and cities of extra attractions, including eating houses, and souvenir shops for the many visitors. The Great Western railway had introduced its first excursion trains during September 1844, running to places such as Bath, Bristol and Exeter. Although these proved to be successful it appears that the Company were slow in exploiting the excursion market to other potential 'tourist' destinations

Using Oxford as an example, the City with its historic University was an obvious destination for the traveller. The line from Didcot Junction to Oxford had been opened on 12 June 1844, but it was not until six years later, in June 1850, that the local Oxford newspaper the *Jackson's Oxford Journal* was moved to comment:

'That although this City has been for many years in connection with the Great Western Railway, it has not up to the present month enjoyed the benefit of a single excursion train … The success of excursion trains on every other railway in the Kingdom has at length opened the eyes of the Great Western Directors to the importance, in a pecuniary point of view,of running excursion trains.'

This criticism obviously had the desired effect as, in August 1850, the first of many Great Western excursions were run into the City. The first 'experimental' excursion from Paddington, Slough, and Reading to Oxford comprising 25 carriages ran on Sunday 18 August 1850, with upwards of 1600 'excursionists' visiting the city. The *Jackson's Oxford Journal* reported that:

'the weather was very favourable, and the excursionists, viewing the various colleges, public buildings, gardens and walks returned at 7 o'clock, highly delighted with what they had seen in this far famed University and City'.

On the following day (Monday) the Great Western ran yet another excursion, this time from Bath and Bristol. This train arrived at Oxford at 10.30am and departed at 7.00pm and comprised 17 carriages and about 900 visitors. The Journal reported that:

'many of the College Halls, Chapels and Gardens were thrown open, and thus the opportunity was afforded of viewing the finest buildings, and promenading in the most beautiful walks in Oxford.'

It was not all good news, as on Sunday 25 August an excursion from Paddington comprising 36 carriages and carrying 2400 passengers arrived some three hours late, due apparently to multiple breakages of coupling chains en route. The *Journal* reported that due to its late arrival 'scarcely anything can be seen here on a Sunday' and that 'the majority went home anything but satisfied with Oxford or the Great Western Railway'. The first ever railway excursion from Oxford to London took place on Monday 2 September 1850. Such was the interest that the train left Oxford with 53 carriages and wagons carrying some 2664 passengers, extra carriages and wagons were added at Abingdon Road (Culham) and at Didcot from where the excursion departed with 58 carriages and wagons carrying some 3,132 passengers. Quite amazing!

From these early days, the Great Western gradually expanded the excursion market and right up until nationalisation and beyond excursion trains formed an important part of both the Great Western and Western Region's revenue.

By the turn of the twentieth century, the Company were looking to speed up passenger services. However there was limit at what could be achieved as services to the South West and South Wales both ran via Bristol, services to Birmingham and beyond ran via Oxford. The Great Western's answer to this problem was to construct a series of 'cut off' lines which would avoid both Bristol and Oxford. To this end, the Great Western constructed three new 'cut offs' in 1903,1906 and 1910 respectively. The first to be opened was the 29¾ mile 'cut off' between Wootton Bassett and Patchway which ran via a 2½ mile tunnel at Sodbury. The new line was opened to passengers on 1 July 1903 and provided a new direct route between London and South Wales, whilst at the same time reducing the distance via Bristol by some 10 miles. Services to the South West were considerably improved when, in June 1906, another new 'cut off' was opened; this ran via Westbury and Castle Cary to Cogload Junction where it joined the old Bristol to Taunton main line. This new line which had been opened in stages

shortened the distance from Paddington to Taunton by some 20 miles. Four years later, on 1 July 1910, the route to Birmingham was also shortened with the opening of yet another new 'cut off' between Ashendon and Aynho Junction, thus reducing the distance between Paddington and Birmingham by some 19 miles. All three new routes allowed considerably faster journey times. It could be said that with the opening of the new 'cut off' routes, the rather derogatory term 'Great Way Round' had probably been removed once and for all. Further work took place in 1933 when new avoiding lines were opened at Westbury and Frome.

New sea routes were opened up or expanded between Weymouth and the Channel Islands and France in August 1889 and to Southern Ireland via Fishguard on 30 August 1906. The new boat trains from Fishguard Harbour were initially timed to complete the 261½ miles in just 5½ hours.

During the First World War, and as an emergency measure, railways in this country were placed into government control. Large numbers of railwaymen from all over the country either enlisted or were conscripted into service. Over the duration of hostilities, the Great Western supplied some 25,479 members of staff which represented about 32% of the pre-war workforce. Of these, some 2,524 were killed, and many others severely wounded. The Locomotive department alone suffered 825 casualties. This obviously placed a great strain on the Great Western to maintain services, with the shortage of manpower being made up by youths, women and older men, many of the latter being retired railwaymen. Each month during this period, the Great Western Magazine religiously published lists of those that were injured or sadly killed in action. In commemoration of the Great Western staff who had given their lives during this conflict, on Armistice day 1922 a War Memorial was unveiled at Paddington Station by the Chairman of the Company, Viscount Churchill. The bronze statue of a soldier was designed and sculptured by Captain C.S. Jagger and stands on platform 1.

An up Ocean Mail special from Plymouth Millbay hauled by a Bulldog 4-4-0 slips coaches at Bedminster Bristol in 1905 The two coaches being slipped are no 837 a 70ft slip storage van,and no 863 a foreign mails van.

St John's Ambulance staff providing tea for the troops at Birmingham Snow Hill in 1916. Many of the St John's staff at this time were volunteer Great Western employees.

In 1915, as part of the war effort, the Great Western constructed two ambulance trains at Swindon for use in France. Both of these trains were sponsored and paid for by the United Kingdom Flower Millers Association. The first train, which was known officially as no 16, comprised seven vehicles; four ward cars, two kitchen cars and one pharmacy coach. The coaches which were essentially 57ft toplight brake thirds and were painted externally in khaki with a large red cross on a white ground on each vehicle. The second ambulance train was known as no. 18 and comprised 16 coaches with accommodation for 482 patients, 144 lying down, 320 sitting up and 18 with infections. There were 45 staff comprising three surgeons, four nurses, six cooks and 32 orderlies. Sadly, such was the need that early in 1916, Swindon constructed a further two 16-coach ambulance trains. In total, some fifteen ambulance trains were constructed at Swindon, comprising some 238 coaches. During their period in service, thousands of allied troops were treated in the trains. After the war, the coaches were placed into store pending sale.

A government report, dated 9 August 1920, stated that 61 of these repatriated coaches were in store and for sale at Didcot. Eventually, many were repurchased by the Great Western and returned to Swindon where they were rebuilt and put back into revenue use, many as excursion coaches.

The austerity of the war years left the railways in a rundown state. On 11 May 1921, a bill was introduced to parliament that would effectively merge all of the country's 120 independent railways in Britain and Northern Ireland into four large Companies. On 19 August 1921, the' Railway Act 1921' was passed, known as the 'Grouping'. The Act which came into force on 1 January 1923, saw the formation of four main operating companies: The Great Western Railway; the Southern Railway; the London Midland & Scottish Railway; and the London & North Eastern Railway.

The grouping saw the Great Western expand even further with the addition of some 32 independent companies. Many of these were in Wales, with the Cambrian Railway, the Taff Vale Railway, the Rhymney Railway, the Barry Railway, the Cardiff Railway and Alexandra

The interior of one of the Continental ambulance trains which were built at Swindon between 1915 and 1916. The two nurses are standing in the ward car of train no 16. The train had accommodation for 144 patients lying down and an equivalent number of 'sitting up' cases. After the war, many of these vehicles were sold back to the Company and were converted to excursion coaches.

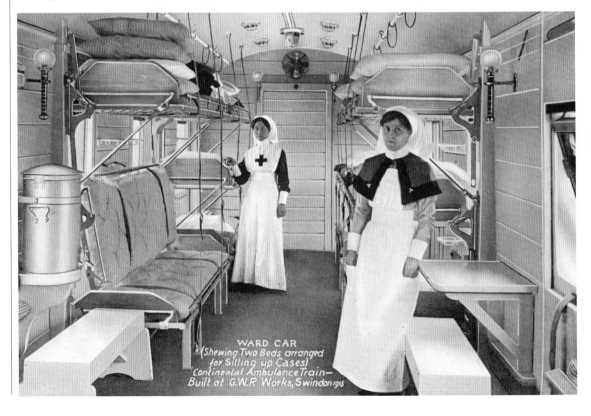

WARD CAR
(Shewing Two Beds arranged for Sitting up Cases)
Continental Ambulance Train—
Built at G.W.R Works, Swindon 1915

Docks railway all becoming Constituent Companies of the GWR, the rest became Subsidiary Companies. These additions also included important docks at Swansea, Barry, Cardiff and Newport.

The result was that almost overnight, the route mileage of the Great Western increased from 3,026 to 3,804, and its total mileage including sidings from 6,645 to 8,993, a far cry from its 1838 total of just 24 miles. From those humble beginnings, the Great Western had grown to become one of the largest and probably the most well-known railway companies in the world. This was helped in no small measure by the fact that the Great Western was the only major company to retain its identity after the Grouping. Subsequently, the 'Great Western' brand became a big selling point in both its passenger and goods services. A year earlier, in 1922, Swindon had started to paint coaching stock in the famous chocolate and cream livery, replacing the overall brown and the classy but rather dull crimson lake livery. The chocolate and cream was a combination that became synonymous with the Great Western and was soon exploited by the publicity department.

Publicity has always played an important part in the operation of the railways in this country. Considering the geographical locations that it served, some of the early publicity used by the Great Western was not particularly inspiring. In 1903, James Inglis became the General Manager and he soon brought improvements to the publicity department. The Great Western started promoting itself as the 'Holiday Line', with posters proclaiming that the Cornish Riviera was 'England's National Health Pleasure Resort'. The term 'The Holiday Line' had been suggested by company employee Archibald Edwards and adopted by the Company in 1908. The South West was an important revenue earner but the Great Western also served other such important holiday destinations such as the Cotswolds, the Thames Valley and Mid and South Wales with the travel advice to 'Go Great Western'.

The famous 'Holiday Haunts' publication listed many of the attractions, together with hotels and guest houses. It was first published in 1894 and continued to be published annually until 1947. In August 1923, the publicity department produced the first of many books, some for 'boys of all ages' included the 10.30 Limited, which described the journey from Paddington to Penzance. This and many other books was the work of Walter George Chapman, a member of the general manager's staff. In 1924, it added to its list of publicity material with the introduction of a series of Jigsaw Puzzles. These were produced by Chad Valley and proved to be particularly popular; between 1924 and 1935 some three-quarters of a million were sold.

Posters were also an important feature of the Company's publicity machine. The first colour posters were poorly designed but as the years went by, they were gradually improved in both content and design using well known artists of the day.

One of the most famous posters was produced in 1939 and I think illustrates the Great Western in its heyday. It depicts King Class locomotive number 6028 *King George V1* on an express service by the artist Charles Mayo and has the wonderfully descriptive heading 'Speed to the West'. Such was its popularity that some 500 copies were also printed for the USA and Canadian market with the title altered to read the 'Great Western Railway of England'.

In 1934, the Great Western rebranded itself with the introduction of the iconic GWR roundel. At the time, this was a very modern design and was soon used on much of the Great Western rolling stock together with the Company's publicity material. It is probably not just a coincidence that the recent rebranding of the 'First Great Western' franchise to 'Great Western Railway' owes something to this 1934 design.

In 1935, the Great Western celebrated the 100th anniversary of the formation of the Company and during the same year it constructed a number of new coaches

In 1934 the Great Western introduced its GWR roundel. It is seen here in this publicity shot of GWR dining car no 9642.

cylinder Castles and Kings, types that were actually based on Churchward's 4-6-0s. These fine locomotives were turned out in fully lined green livery, with copper capped chimneys and safety valve bonnets, features that caught the public's attention and helped promote 'God's Wonderful Railway' as the way to travel. Speed was always a feature of Great Western services and it was during the 1920s/30s that the company held the record for the fastest non- stop run with its famous 'Cheltenham Flyer' service, in 1932, this service was timed to run the 77.3 miles from Swindon to Paddington in just 65 minutes. The service that became synonymous with the Great Western was the famous 'Cornish Riviera Express'. Departing from Paddington at 10.30am, it was for many years powered by Collett's King Class 4-6-0s. The service had essentially started on 1 July 1904 with the introduction of the first regular non-stop run between Paddington and Plymouth; its introduction ensured that for many years the Company had the distinction of holding the record for the longest daily non-stop train in the world.

Over the years, the Great Western's motive power policy had been to build locomotives that were essentially 'horses for courses', and this continued even after nationalisation when the newly formed Western Region continued to construct Swindon designed locomotives to operate its services and to replace ageing motive power. Between February 1948 and December 1950, some thirty Castles, forty-nine Modified Halls and ten Manor Class 4-6-0s were constructed at Swindon. Added to this list are twenty 5101 Class 2-6-2Ts and some 321 0-6-0PTs, all built between April 1948 and May 1955 at Swindon, and by outside contractors.

The Great Western was generally a very safe railway, and between 1905 and 1928 there were no mishaps on passenger services that resulted in loss of life; this was due in no small measure to the maintenance of the stock and the diligence of the staff. Safety had been further

ostensibly for use on the Cornish Riviera Express. The new 'Centenary' coaches were 9ft 7in wide and 60ft long and were fitted with recessed doors. Their size unfortunately restricted them over many routes, but with a King or a Castle in charge, the new Centenary stock looked magnificent. It also was during this period that services were speeded up, and for the Summer service in 1938 there were no less than 42 express passenger services timed to run at 58mph or more from start to stop.

From the early 1900s, passenger services had been getting heavier with longer and faster trains. Many of these services required double-heading, a costly exercise taking up two locomotives and double the number of crews. The urgent need was for new and more powerful locomotives. Churchward proved to be the right man at the right time, designing his famous 2 cylinder Saint and 4 cylinder Star Class 4-6-0s. These fine locomotives were capable of hauling both heavier and faster services over many of the main lines without the requirement of 'double heading'. Churchward was followed by Collett with his even more powerful 4

improved with the introduction of the Automatic Train Control system. ATC had first been introduced by the Great Western in 1906, as an experiment on the Twyford to Henley and the Oxford to Fairford branches. The system proved successful and in 1908 it was installed on the Great Western main line between Slough and Reading. Initially, the system just provided a warning in the cab if a signal was approached at caution, but in 1912, it was modified to include an automatic brake application. ATC as it was known became great safety aid, by 1930 it had been introduced to cover some 370 miles and from 1930 it was gradually extended over the whole system and from that date all new built locomotives were fitted with ATC equipment.

The Second World War saw the Great Western again supply a large number of its staff to the military. However, during this second conflict, those away in service were mainly replaced by women. Great Western records indicate that up to 16,000 women were employed by the Company over the war period. In 1945, the Chairman of the Great Western, Sir Charles Hambro,

reported that 15,000 employees had served in the forces or in full time Civil Defence posts and that 444 were killed in action, 155 were reported missing and a further 271 were reported as prisoners of war or interned in neutral countries. Once again, the casualties were reported each month in the *Great Western Magazine*. During this conflict, the Great Western also suffered extensive bomb damage at many locations with Bristol, Weymouth, Plymouth, Birmingham and London as well as the docks in South Wales affected. On Friday 11 November 1949, the War Memorial at Paddington was rededicated by Sir James Milne when a further 794 names of staff that lost their lives during the Second World War were added.

It is interesting to note that from its inception right up to the start of the Second World War, the Company had paid a dividend to its shareholders of not less than 3%. The Great Western had performed well during the war and had certainly 'done its bit', but after hostilities had ceased and with a lack of investment, the railway system in this country was in a run-down state. In 1945, a new Labour

King Class 4-6-0 no 6012 *King Edward V1* on the down 'Cornish Riviera' service is pictured here on Westbury loop on 30 March 1936. The train is formed of 'Centenary' stock. Twenty-six of these coaches were built at Swindon during 1935 especially for this service.

The Great Western suffered considerable bomb damage during the Second World War. This is the remains of the booking office at Bristol Temple Meads after one such raid on 5 January 1941.

'Soldier comes home', by Great Western of course. A wonderful publicity shot taken at an unknown Great Western station in June 1944.

government was elected under the leadership of Clement Attlee. In its election manifesto was the pledge to nationalise the transport system in this country. Accordingly, in 1947, a new Transport Act was passed by parliament which saw the railways, road transport and the ailing canal system nationalised and placed under the control of the newly formed British Transport Commission. A second tier of management, the Railway Executive (RE), was formed at the same time, and as its name implies was responsible for the railways. On 1 January 1948, five new regions were formed: Western Region; Southern Region; London Midland Region; Eastern Region; and Scottish Region. Interestingly out of the five new regions, the Western Region was the only one to retain its locomotive numbering system, probably due in some measure to the cost of replacing the unique brass and cast iron number plates. Accordingly, on 1 January, some 3,803 locomotives, 8,293 coaching vehicles, 86,170 goods wagons and 9,460 service vehicles passed from Great Western to Western Region control. The rolling stock, together with the infrastructure, was of course still pure Great Western, and most if not all of the workforce were still ex-Great Western men and women. It is because of this that the traditions of the old company lived on, probably right up until the end of steam traction in 1965. As the saying goes 'a Leopard does not change his spots overnight', and even after Nationalisation the Western Region was known by many as the Great Western Region, but to others it was and still is known as 'God's Wonderful Railway'.

It is truly remarkable just how much of Brunel's influence has survived and can still be clearly seen today at Paddington, Bristol Temple Meads and at smaller stations such as Frome and Culham. His major engineering work at Maidenhead Bridge, Sonning, Box Tunnel, the Royal Albert Bridge, and of course the Great Western main line itself bear testimony to his genius.

BROAD GAUGE LOCOMOTIVES

The line from Paddington to Maidenhead was opened on 4 June 1838 and on 30 March 1840, it reached Reading. Initially, the Company had purchased twenty locomotives from various manufacturers to operate the services, but many of these proved to be unreliable. Brunel, for all of his engineering prowess, was not so good when it came to choosing locomotives for the new railway, and those that were supplied to his specification by the various manufactures fell well short of what was required. Failures were the norm rather than the exception. The appointment of 21 year old Daniel Gooch on 18 August 1837 proved to be a master stroke as he almost single-handedly kept these unreliable locomotives going during these early years. The only locomotive to come up to scratch was the Robert Stephenson designed 2-2-2 *North Star*; this had been previously built for the 5ft 6in gauge New Orleans Railway but when that contract was cancelled it was sold to the Great Western and converted to 7ft 0¼in gauge. Reliability soon improved with the construction of twelve of the Star class 2-2-2s, and sixty-two of the equally reliable Firefly Class 2-2-2 locomotives, the latter being constructed by no less than seven different manufacturers. Purchasing locomotives was a costly

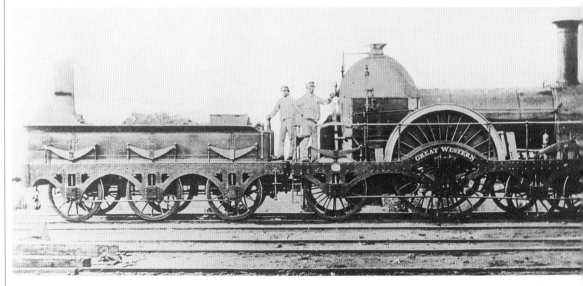

The first locomotive to be entirely built at Swindon was the Gooch designed 2-2-2 *Great Western*, which was completed in April 1846. On 1st June 1846, it covered the 194 miles from Paddington to Exeter in just 208 minutes running time. The run back to Paddington was equally as swift being accomplished in 211 minutes. Another fast run took place on 13 June 1846, with a 100 ton load. The 77 miles from Paddington to Swindon was completed in just 78 minutes, a fast run indeed. Unfortunately, it suffered a broken leading axle whilst working a service near Shrivenham and during the same year it was rebuilt as a 4-2-2. It is pictured here, probably in the 1850s; notice the 'iron coffin' guard's shelter on the rear of the tender. *Great Western* was withdrawn in December 1870, having amassed 370,687 miles in service.

Firefly Class 2-2-2 *Saturn* was built by R.B. Longridge and Co at their Bedlington works in June 1841 and is pictured here as rebuilt at Swindon in October 1864 and with the later added cab. It was withdrawn from service in June 1878 and sold by the Great Western to the Metropolitan Board of Works.

An early shot of Victoria Class 2-4-0 *Telford*, this was a sixth lot passenger locomotive built at Swindon in April 1864. Like many of these early locomotives it did not have long life, being withdrawn in February 1879.

business, and it soon became obvious to the Company that it would be far better to design and construct their own. To this end, in 1840 the company decided to construct a locomotive works at Swindon. The new works opened in January 1843, initially for repairs to the existing fleet, but later for construction.

Gooch 'standard goods' class 0-6-0 *Liffey* was built at Swindon in August 1857 and withdrawn in March 1872. It was one of 102 standard goods locomotives that were built at Swindon between May 1852 and March 1863. None of these early types were fitted with engine brakes.

The ex- South Devon Railway 0-6-0ST no 2165 *Achilles* seen here at Penzance in broad gauge days. One of ten 0-6-0 goods engines built by the Avonside Engine Company in December 1873, it was converted to standard gauge in July 1893 and renumbered 1324. It was withdrawn and sold to the South Wales Mineral Railway's Glyncorrwg Colliery in April 1905 becoming no 7. The grouping in 1923 saw it return to Great Western stock being numbered 818. It was withdrawn in May 1932.

Rover Class 4-2-2 *Swallow* stands in the yard at Bristol Bath Road. The 24 locomotives of the 'Rover' class were officially listed as rebuilds or renewals but were essentially new locomotives that replaced the earlier locomotives of the same name. The original *Swallow* was built at Swindon in June 1849 and was withdrawn in September 1871. The new *Swallow* seen here was built in September 1871 and was withdrawn from service with the end of the broad gauge on 20 May 1892. On the left is the original Bristol and Exeter locomotive shed and on the right, the famous clock tower leading to the turntable and the 1877 standard gauge roundhouse. The whole shed complex was demolished and rebuilt between 1931 and 1934

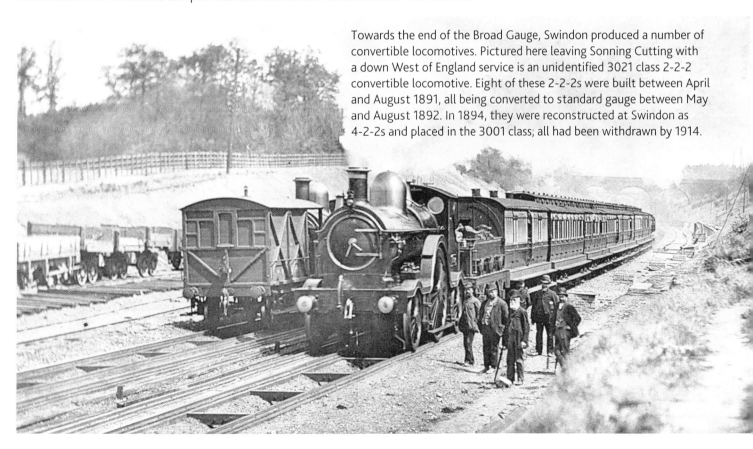

Towards the end of the Broad Gauge, Swindon produced a number of convertible locomotives. Pictured here leaving Sonning Cutting with a down West of England service is an unidentified 3021 class 2-2-2 convertible locomotive. Eight of these 2-2-2s were built between April and August 1891, all being converted to standard gauge between May and August 1892. In 1894, they were reconstructed at Swindon as 4-2-2s and placed in the 3001 class; all had been withdrawn by 1914.

The Great Western preserved just two broad gauge locomotives, Gooch single 4-2-2 *Lord of the Isles* together with the 2-2-2 *North Star*. The two locomotives were placed in store at Swindon, but with space apparently at a premium unbelievably, in January 1906, they were both cut up. However, the 8ft flangeless driving wheels from *Lord of the Isles* were saved and are seen here at Faverdale Works, Darlington, in September 1925, being prepared for display at the Stockton and Darlington Centenary Exhibition.

A replica *North Star* was built at Swindon in 1925 especially for display at the exhibition. The replica is seen here at Faverdale after arriving from Swindon on 'Crocodile' wagon no 41914. The information board on the right explains the history of *North Star* but interestingly does not mention that it is a replica. After the exhibition, *North Star* was placed on display inside Swindon A shop.

NINETEENTH AND TWENTIETH CENTURY STANDARD GAUGE LOCOMOTIVES

Over the whole period of its existence, the Great Western had just six locomotive superintendents: Daniel Gooch (Loco Supt) from August 1837-October 1864; Joseph Armstrong (Loco and Carriage Supt) from January 1864-June 1877 (Armstrong was initially the locomotive superintendent at Wolverhampton taking over Gooch's role on his retirement); William Dean (Loco and Carriage Supt) between June 1877 and June 1902; George Jackson Churchward from June 1902 until December 1921; Charles B Collett from January 1922 until July 1941 and last but not least, Frederick Hawksworth from July 1941 until December 1947. The post of Locomotive Superintendent was altered to Chief Mechanical Engineer in 1916.

The Armstrong 322 or 'Beyer' class 0-6-0s were an early standard gauge design. No 338 was built in December 1864 and was one of thirty locomotives designed and built by Beyer Peacock & Co between 1864 and 1866. It is seen here with a W3 type boiler that it received in February 1883. It was withdrawn in August 1924. Notice the large locomotive jack on the running board; these were carried by many locomotives at this time.

'Chancellor' or 'England' Class 2-4-0 no 153 was built by George England & Co at their Hatcham Ironworks in Kent in August 1862. One of a class of eight that were ordered by Gooch, they were the first 2-4-0s built for the standard gauge. All eight were renewed between 1878 and 1883. No 153, seen here at Chester, was renewed in June 1882 and was withdrawn in May 1907.

Armstrong Standard Goods 0-6-0 no 31 was built at Swindon in February 1872 and withdrawn in February 1905. These attractive outside frame locomotives worked over the whole system and were gradually replaced by the later Dean designed goods 0-6-0s. Notice how the coal is piled up on the tender which has no side fenders.

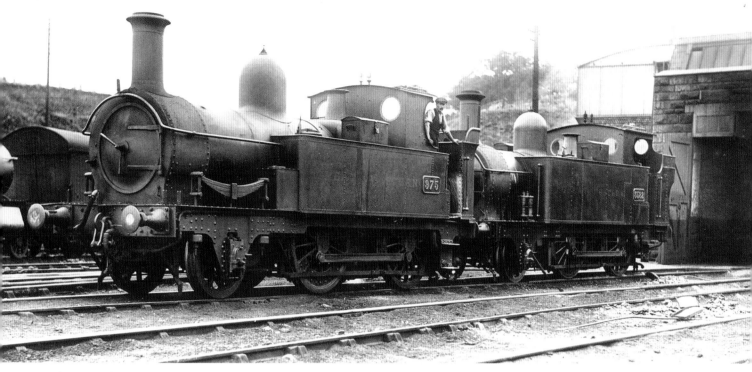

A pair of Metropolitan class 2-4-0Ts stand at Truro shed on 4 August 1926. 140 of these 2-4-0Ts were constructed between 1869 and 1899 and were used on both branch and suburban services over the system. No 975 was built at Swindon September 1874 and is seen here with an open cab. No 3582 was constructed in February 1899 and has an enclosed cab and larger capacity side tanks. 975 was withdrawn in April 1934, and 3582 in November 1949.

No 2026 was a 2021 class 0-6-0ST built at Wolverhampton in May 1897. In September 1922, it was altered to a Pannier tank, as seen here at Swindon on 17 January 1930, coupled to the Great Western four wheeled inspection saloon no 80974. This vehicle was built for the Bristol & Exeter Railway as a 6 wheeled 1st/2nd class composite coach with two toilets. It was converted to an inspection saloon by the Great Western by mounting the modified body onto a longer 4 wheeled underframe and numbered 472, later 6472. In September 1921, it was renumbered once again 80974. No 2026 was withdrawn in April 1951.

There is no doubt that the Gooch 8ft singles of the broad gauge era were particularly fine looking locomotives, but I would argue that probably the most elegant locomotives to run on the Great Western were the 7ft 8in Dean 3031 class 4-2-2s. Here no 3050 *Royal Sovereign* waits to depart from Paddington with a down express service in around 1902. For many years, the locomotive was used to haul the Royal Train. Built at Swindon in February 1895, it is seen here fitted with a special coiled spring bogie. *Royal Sovereign* was withdrawn in December 1915.

Duke Class 4-4-0 no 3288 *Tresco* stands in the yard at Weymouth in 1901. Designed by Dean and built at Swindon in 1897, it was renumbered 3277 and renamed *Isle of Tresco* in February 1904. The cleaners pattern (quivering) can be clearly seen on the locomotive and tender. No 3277 was withdrawn in January 1937.

Bulldog class 4-4-0 no 3405 *Empire of India* stands in the yard at Reading in the 1930s. The Bulldog class were introduced by Dean in 1899, no 3405 was built in March 1904 and is seen here fitted with a superheater and top feed. It was withdrawn in April 1937.

The Great Western produced some odd designs over the years one of which was Dean 'Badminton' Class 4-4-0 no 3297 *Earl Cawdor*, passing Acton with the 10.15am milk train. Built in May 1898, in July 1903 it was fitted with an S4X large experimental round top boiler and a double side windowed cab which gave the locomotive more of a North Eastern (rather) than Great Western look. The cab was replaced by a standard Churchward open cab in November 1904, and after a number of boiler changes, the locomotive was withdrawn as no 4105 in November 1927.

The 'Aberdare Class 2-6-0s were introduced in 1900. The class were mainly used on coal trains, but in later years could be seen on both mineral trains and general goods. No 2650 passes through Ruabon in around 1932 with a class F express goods service. No 2650 was built in December 1901 and withdrawn in May 1936.

The 2301 class Dean Goods 0-6-0s were arguably the most successful of the Dean designs. They operated over much of the system, with a number being used by the War Department in both world wars. Several members of the class continued in use until the 1950s. No 2467 was built in January 1896; notice the fully lined tender full of enormous lumps of coal. It was withdrawn in October 1940.

Dean 3521 class 0-4-4T no 3537 stands at Exeter St Davids. It has double lining and a hand painted 'Newton Abbot Division' on the tool box. No 3537 was built as a 0-4-2T in February 1888 it was altered to an 0-4-4T as seen here in March 1892. As 0-4-4Ts, the class gained a reputation as being unstable and to rectify this they were altered once more into 4-4-0 tender locomotives, no 3537 being altered in May 1899, and in this guise the much altered locomotive continued in service until its withdrawal in September 1928.

A 517 class 0-4-2T no 1473 *Fair Rosamund,* seen here at Oxford in around 1910. Built at Wolverhampton in May 1883. 156 class 517 locomotives were built at Wolverhampton between 1868 and 1885. It is pictured here with an open cab, which it carried until 1924 when it was fitted with an enclosed cab. It was apparently named *Fair Rosamund* in 1896 for working a royal train over the Woodstock (Blenheim) branch. It carried its nameplate until withdrawal in August 1935. It was an unusual choice for a name as *Fair Rosamund* was a mistress of Henry II and lived in a 'bower' near Woodstock that had been specially built for her by the king.

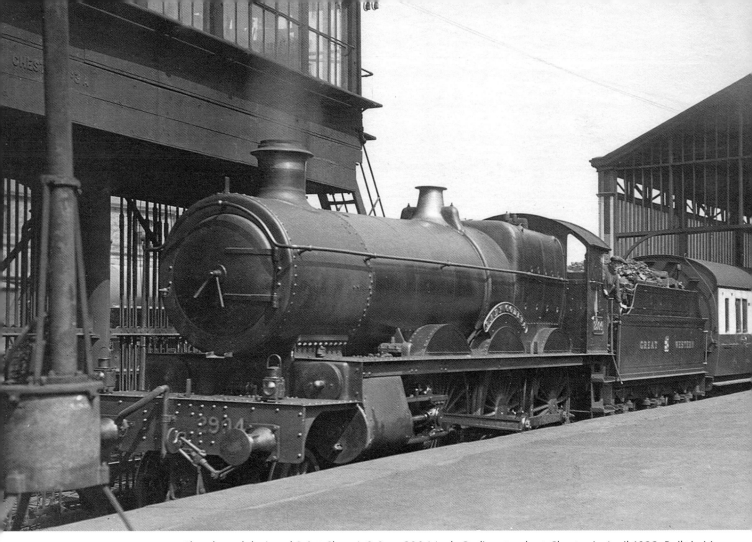

Churchward designed Saint Class 4-6-0 no 2904 *Lady Godiva* stands at Chester in April 1932. Built in May 1906, it was fitted with a superheater in July 1910 and is pictured here with top feed and a tall safety valve bonnet. It was withdrawn in October 1932.

Together with the 2 cylinder Saints, the 4 cylinder Star class 4-6-0s were probably the most successful locomotives in the country during the first half of the twentieth century. Pictured here on the sea wall at Teignmouth is no 4021 *King Edward* with an up fast service to London. Built at Swindon in June 1909 it was renamed *The British Monarch* in June 1927 and *British Monarch* in October 1927. It was withdrawn from Oxford in October 1952.

It was said that in their day the 2800 class 2-8-0s were the best heavy freight locomotives in this country. Some 167 members of the class were built between 1903 and 1942. In 1906, no 2808 on a special test train set a new haulage record for a British steam locomotive, when it hauled 107 loaded wagons weighing 2012 tons including a dynamometer car and brake van between Swindon and Acton. Pictured here is no 3825 on a mixed freight service approaching Sonning, east of Reading, in 1946. As a wartime measure it has its side windows blanked off. Built at Swindon in September 1940, it was withdrawn by the Western Region in September 1964.

Churchward designed 3100 class 2-6-2 no 5126 on a fast passenger service near Flax Bourton in April 1937. Built as no 3126 in June 1905, it was renumbered 5126 in August 1929 and withdrawn in October 1938.

Churchward designed the 4300 class 2-6-0s 'Moguls' in 1911. They were essentially a tender version of his 3150 class 2-6-2T and proved to be one of the most successful of the many Great Western classes. Some 342 locomotives were built between 1911 and 1932 being used on almost all types of service over the system. Pictured here at Torquay in September 1932 is no 8342, waiting to depart on an up service. Built as no.5342 in February 1918, it was rebuilt in January 1928 with extra weight at the front end to improve stability and renumbered 8342, and in this guise it stayed until its withdrawal in April 1937.

No 4705 rounds the sea wall at Teignmouth with an up passenger service. Nine of these fine 2-8-0 locomotives were built at Swindon between 1919 and 1923 mainly for use on overnight fitted express freight services, but as seen here they were often used during the summer months on passenger services to and from the South West. No 4705 was constructed in April 1922 and withdrawn in December 1963. The Great Western Society are currently constructing a replica 4700 class at Didcot.

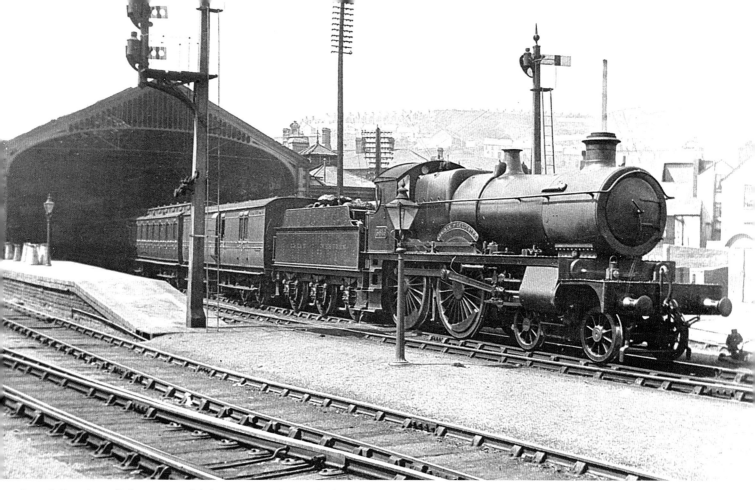

One of Churchward's less successful designs were the 2 cylinder 4-4-0 County Class. No 3816 *County of Leicester* is seen here at Plymouth North Road in the 1920s. Built in December 1906, it was withdrawn in September 1931.The County Class 4-4-0s were acknowledged by the crews to be rough riders.

The Small Prairie 4500 class 2-6-2Ts were designed to operate over many of the branch lines on the Great Western system. They were essentially a scaled down version of the 3100 class 2-6-2Ts. Pictured here at St Erth on 28 August 1936 is no 4503 on the 11.13am service to St Ives. No 4503 was built at Wolverhampton in January 1907, and withdrawn from service in January 1951.

The 1361 Class 0-6-0ST were built at Swindon in 1910 primarily for dock work at Plymouth and Weymouth. No 1362 was built in June 1910 and is seen here at Newton Abbot in September 1932, after a visit to the works for a light repair. It was withdrawn from Taunton in May 1961. No 1363 of the same class is preserved at Didcot Railway Centre.

Collett took over the post of Chief Mechanical Engineer from Churchward on 1 January 1922. He soon Introduced a number of new types of 4-6-0 express passenger and mixed traffic locomotives. In doing so he based his designs on Churchward's very successful 2 cylinder Saint and 4 cylinder Star class 4-6-0s. The Castles appeared in 1923, the larger King Class in 1927 and the mixed traffic Hall class in 1928. His Grange and Manor class 2 cylinder 4-6-0s were introduced between 1936 and 1939.

The Castles proved to be fast and reliable locomotives. No 5006, *Tregenna Castle,* built in June 1927, stands at Old Oak Common in the 1930s. This locomotive was used on the 3.48pm 'Cheltenham Flyer' service on 6 June 1932 when it covered the 77.30 miles from Swindon to Paddington in just 56minutes and 47 seconds at an average speed of 81.6 mph, thus securing the world record for the fastest start to stop run. It was withdrawn in April 1962.

For over 30 years, the Kings reigned supreme on the heavy services over the cut-off route from Paddington to Birkenhead. The majestic sight of the 2.10pm service from Paddington to Birkenhead climbing the bank at Saunderton in 1932 hauled by no 6017 *King Edward IV*. Built in June 1928 it was withdrawn in July 1962.

Another of Collett's successful locomotive types were the 2 cylinder Hall Class 4-6-0s. These were based on Churchward's 2 cylinder Saint Class 4-6-0s. Pictured here at Old Oak Common is no 4900 *Saint Martin*. This was the prototype locomotive for the Hall class being rebuilt from Saint class no 2925 in 1924. It ran as 2925 *Saint Martin* until it was renumbered 4900 in December 1928.

The Grange Class 4-6-0s were excellent mixed traffic locomotives, with 80 members of the class being built between 1936 and 1939.Pictured here is an almost new no 6802 Bampton Grange on a parcels service at Bentley Heath Crossing on 19 September 1936. No 6802 entered traffic on 3 September 1936 and was withdrawn from service on 7 October 1961.

The 6100 class 2-6-2T were designed by Collet but were basically a modern version of Churchward's 3100 class 2-6-2T. The majority of the seventy members of the class were to be seen on suburban services in the Thames Valley area. No 6112 passes Kensal Green gas works in the 1930s with a down Thames Valley suburban service comprising a six coach articulated suburban set. Built in August 1931, no 6112 was withdrawn in September 1965.

The 5400 class 0-6-0s were built between 1931 and 1935,they were all auto-fitted for working branch auto-train services. No 5417 stands at North Acton on 28 June 1947 on the last day of the Greenford to Westbourne Park service. It was withdrawn in January 1961.

A pair of 4800 class 0-4-2T s no's 4805 and 4851 stand in the loco yard at Exeter St Davids in 1938. Designed by Collett for branch line use to replace the ageing 517 class locomotives, no 4805 was constructed at Swindon in September 1932 and retains the earlier 'Great Western' logo on its tank. No 4851 was built in July 1935 and has the later GWR roundel on its tank. All of the 4800 class 0-4-2Ts were renumbered in the 1400 sequence during 1946. No 4805 was withdrawn September 1958, and 4851 in July 1964.

Although it was the larger 4-6-0s that got the limelight, it was the small shunting locomotives that provided the backbone of the railway. Pictured here on a mixed goods service at Kensington Addison Road is no 8770, one of 863 members of the 5700 and 8750 class 0-6-0PTs built for the Great Western and the Western Region between 1929 and 1950. No 8770 was built in January 1934 and was withdrawn in December 1962.

Hawksworth took over from Collett in July 1941, his first design was the Modified Hall class, a development of Collett's Hall class. The Modified Halls were very successful and standing in the yard at Old Oak Common is No 6974 *Bryngwyn Hall* built at Swindon in October 1947. It was withdrawn from service in May 1965.

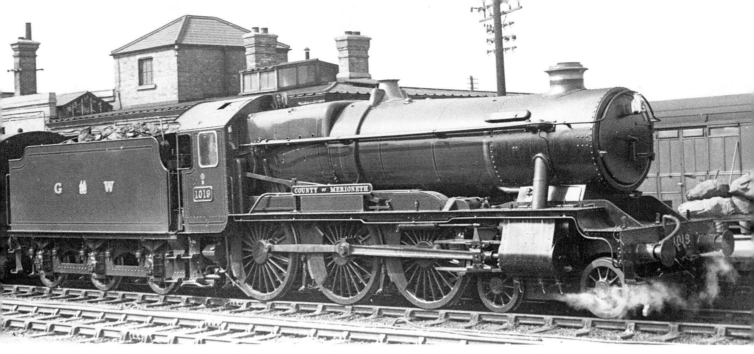

The County Class 4-6-0s were introduced in 1945, and were the most powerful 2 cylinder 4-6-0s on the Great Western.In 1954 and after a number of tests, the class were gradually fitted with double chimneys which greatly improved their performance. No 1019 *County of Merioneth,* stands at Swindon on a running in turn to Didcot on 4 April 1946. It had been completed at the works just a few days previously and has the post war Hawksworth style Great Western logo on the tender. It was fitted with a double chimney in March 1959 and withdrawn in February 1963.

Hawksworth also designed the 9400 class 0-6-0PTs.These were fitted with taper boilers and were designed for heavy shunting duties. The first 10 were constructed at Swindon in 1947, no 9401 is pictured here at Paddington on station pilot duties; it carries the post war gold sans-serif GWR edged in black. A further 200 of the Hawksworth 9400 0-6-0PTs were constructed for the Western Region between 1949 and 1956 by a number of private contractors.

STEAM RAILMOTORS

The Great Western introduced its first steam rail motors on services between Chalford and Stonehouse on 12 October 1903. The steam rail motor proved to be an ideal form of motive power at this time and were used on many branch lines, and also some suburban services. On many routes new Halts were opened to accommodate the steam rail motor services. For example in the Oxford area alone Halts were opened on 1 February 1908 at Wolvercote, Hinksey, Abingdon Road, Iffley, Garsington Bridge and at Horspath.

Such was the popularity of the rail motors that a total of 99 were built between 1903 and 1908. Although they were initially successful, from around 1914 they were gradually withdrawn and replaced by auto-trains. One of the problems with the steam rail motor if there was a breakdown then the whole unit had to be taken out of service. The auto-trains had been introduced by the Great Western as early as 1905 by fitting auto gear to a number of the 517 class 0-4-2Ts. The steam rail motor halts in the Oxford area were all closed by 1916. The very last

An early shot of steam rail motor no 2 at Chalford. No 2 was built in October 1903 and withdrawn in January 1917. This was the first steam rail motor service to be introduced by the Great Western and a report of the time states that their introduction saw an increase in passenger numbers over the route of nearly 600%.

steam rail motor service operated between Neath (Canal side) and Court Sart being withdrawn on 16 September 1935. Many of the withdrawn rail motors survived the cutter's torch being converted into trailer cars. Luckily, one of these steam rail motors survives at Didcot Railway Centre. No 93 was built in 1908 and was withdrawn and converted to auto trailer no 212 in 1935. It was withdrawn in May 1956 but was luckily retained by British Rail for use as a work study coach. It was purchased from BR and brought to Didcot in 1970. In 2011, the Great Western Society with lottery funding converted no 212 back to steam rail motor no.93, the work entailing amongst other things, the construction of a brand new power bogie.

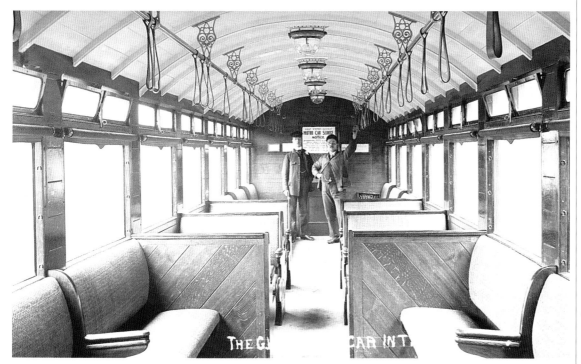

The interior of one of the first two steam rail motors, pictured here whilst on a Chalford to Stonehouse service.

A postcard view showing Rail motor no 90 at Newquay, taken probably some time before the First World War on a service to Truro via Perranporth. No 90 was built in December 1907 and withdrawn in December 1927.

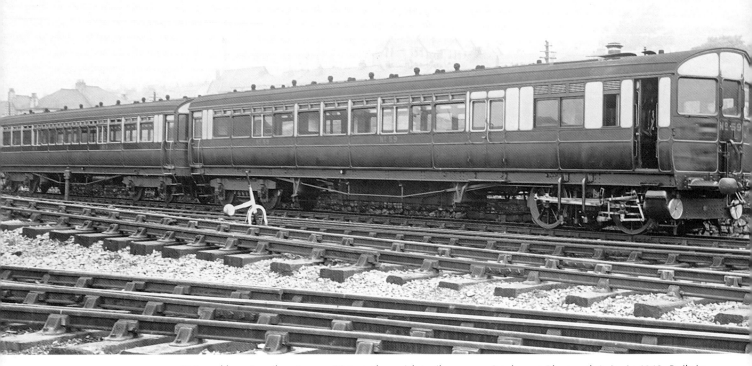

Pictured here is rail motor no 59 together with trailer car no 9 taken at Plymouth Laira in 1913. Built in August 1905, it was withdrawn in June 1920.

Passengers pose for the photographer at Stanley Bridge Halte in 1905. The service is being operated by rail motor no 19, which was allocated to Chippenham between February and September 1905. Built in July 1904, it was withdrawn in August 1919. The Halte was situated on the Chippenham to Calne branch. The word Halte is derived from contemporary French (stop) and although used in a number of other locations on the Great Western the 'E' was soon dropped from the name.

Rail motor no 46 and trailer coach are seen here on the Chippenham to Calne branch rounding the curve near Hazeland, in around 1911. No 46 was built in February 1905 and withdrawn in November 1922.

GWR PETROL AND DIESEL VEHICLES

Simplex no 15 was a petrol powered shunter built by the Motor Rail and Tram Company Ltd of Bedford in April 1923 and taken into Great Western stock soon after. It is seen here possibly at Wolverhampton, with, in the background, steam railmotor no 86. No 15 was withdrawn and cut up at Swindon in 1951. The Great Western purchased a further four Simplex locomotives between 1926 and 1927, all of which survived until 1960. It was during the 1930s that the GWR first experimented with the use of heavy oil (diesel) traction.

In April 1933, the Company purchased an 0-4-0 Diesel mechanical shunter from John Fowler and Co of Leeds. Given the number 1, it is seen here at Swindon probably soon after delivery and in Great Western middle chrome lined green livery. It was interestingly also fitted with an auxiliary petrol engine that was used for starting purposes. At Swindon, it was used on shunting duties within the works. It was sold in March 1940 to Geo Cohen, Sons and Co Ltd Leeds, and then onwards to the Ministry of Supply.

In April 1936 the Great Western purchased a second shunting locomotive, this time from R &W Hawthorn, Leslie and Co Ltd. It was numbered 2 and is pictured here in full lined green livery at Swindon in 1936. No 2 proved to be a successful and a reliable design. It was renumbered 15100 in the BR scheme in March 1948 and after spending many years at Bristol St Phillip's Marsh, it was withdrawn from Swindon in April 1965.

On 4 December 1933, Great Western took delivery of the first of its famous 'Streamlined' diesel railcars. These diesel mechanical railcars were built by AEC Ltd at Southall, with the first four having bodywork constructed by Park Royal Coachworks Ltd. The railcars were to be seen over many parts of the system; in 1947 for example, the 37 surviving members of the class were allocated to 14 different locomotive depots. Well after nationalisation, they continued to give good use, with the last examples not being withdrawn until October 1962. This publicity postcard shows Diesel Railcar no 1 standing at Southall. It was first put into service on 4 December 1933, running on local services between Paddington and Reading. Fitted with a single AEC diesel engine, it had a top speed of 60mph. It was taken out of service for a number of modifications including improvements to the braking system and at the same time it was fitted with Automatic Train Control. It returned to service on 5 February 1934 and was withdrawn in August 1955.

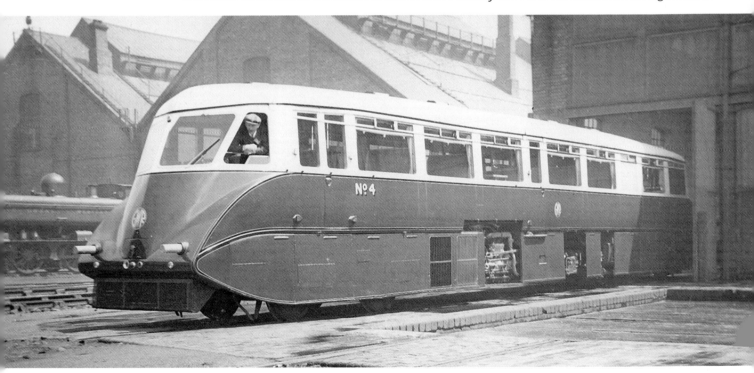

AEC Railcar no 4 stands outside the works at Old Oak Common in 1936. No 4 entered service on 26 September 1934. This railcar, together with nos 2 and 3, were fitted with a pair of AEC diesel engines which gave a top speed of 75-80 mph. All three were fitted with a buffet bar and toilets, and until about 1940 were used on express business services between Birmingham and Cardiff. No 4 was withdrawn in July 1958 and is now preserved as part of the National Collection

GWR the Streamline way

Cover of pamphlet issued by the Great Western in July 1934 for the inauguration of the new business service between Birmingham and Cardiff on 16 July.

One of the new railcars, probably no 2, is a source of interest at Cardiff on 16 July 1934 after arriving with the newly introduced buffet service from Birmingham. No 2 entered service on 9 July 1934 and was withdrawn in February 1954.

Between 1933 and 1942 some 38 diesel railcars were constructed for the Great Western but from Railcar no 5 construction of the bodies switched to the Gloucester Railway Carriage and Wagon Company. No 17 was turned out as a parcels vehicle and was placed into stock in April 1936. It is pictured here at Sonning on a down parcels service possibly soon after its construction. On the main line is Castle no 5046 Earl Cawdor on a down fast service. No 17 was withdrawn in January 1959.

From railcar no 19 a more angular design was adopted. Waiting at Tintern on a Wye Valley service in September 1946 is no 23. It was constructed in September 1940 and is seen here in the post war Hawksworth GWR livery. It was withdrawn in October 1962.

Rail car nos 35 and 36 were constructed as twin units in November 1941 and are pictured here soon after construction on the Brentford branch. In later years and to increase capacity a standard passenger coach was inserted between the two units. Both were withdrawn in April 1957.

OIL BURNING

In the autumn of 1945, the Great Western, in collaboration with the Anglo-Iranian Oil Company, started a programme to convert a number of 2800 class heavy freight 2-8-0s to burn oil. In preparation for this, large capacity oil storage tanks were installed at a number of depots. The first locomotive to be converted was no 2872 (renumbered 4800 in the oil burning series) in October 1945. The experiment was extended to include some Hall and Castle class 4-6-0 locomotives. The original intention was to convert 85 Halls, 25 Castle class 4-6-0s, and 73 2800 class 2-8-0s and for some reason just a single 4300 class 2-6-0. What became an expensive exercise was abandoned in 1949, with just thirty-seven Great Western locomotives being converted, and by April 1950, all of these had been converted back to burn coal.

2800 class 2-8-0 no 4801 (2854) is seen here being refuelled at Severn Tunnel Junction in January 1947. The large oil tank was placed in the coal hopper of the Churchward 3,500 gallon tender. No 4801 was converted back to burn coal in February 1949.

A great shot of no 4807 (2848) on a heavy freight. It was one of just twenty 2800 class 2-8-0s that were converted to burn oil between October 1945 and September 1947.No 4807 was converted to oil in June 1947, reverting back to coal in July 1949.

No 4948 *Northwick Hall* was converted in May 1947 and was renumbered 3902. It is seen here on an up fast service soon after conversion. It was converted back to burn coal in September 1948.

No 100A1 Lloyds was one of five Castles to be converted. It is seen here with Hall no 6947 *Helmingham Hall* on a down fast service near Slough on 10 June 1947. The Castle was converted back to coal in September 1948.

The only 4300 class 2-6-0 to be converted to oil was no 6320 in March 1947. It is seen here departing from Gloucester on 26 April 1947. No 6320 was not renumbered in the oil burning series and was converted back to coal in August 1949.

ENGINE SHEDS

ngine sheds large and small were an important part of the operation of railways in this country. In 1938, the Great Western had an operating fleet of some 3,630 locomotives, that were needed to haul the many main and branch line services over the system, and also to provide shunting locomotives for the many goods yards and depots. In 1938 these locomotives were allocated between 61 main line locomotive sheds and 86 sub-sheds. All of these provided the basic requirement of coal and water, with many of the larger sheds also providing maintenance and repairs. The staff at these sheds worked long hours under arduous and dirty conditions.

The interior of Old Oak Common taken soon after it opened in 17 March 1906. This was the largest engine shed on the Great Western and replaced the old broad gauge sheds at Westbourne Park. The new shed complex was designed by G J Churchward and comprised four large roundhouses, two of which can be seen in this picture. Notice the extra safety feature of boarded over turntables. Locomotives in view are from L to R) Saint Class no 2915 *Saint Bartholomew*, Bulldog 4-4-0 no 3391 *Dominion of Canada*, Star class 4-6-0 no 4003 *Lode Star* and an unidentified 3031 class 4-2-2. Old Oak remained the largest engine shed on the Great Western and later the Western Region,il closed to steam on 22 March 1965.

The Great Western shed at Chester in August 1933. A brick built shed was opened here in 1856 and was rebuilt in 1928; at this time it had an allocation of 51 locomotives. It was closed to steam in April 1960.

Exeter in the 1930s; on the left outside the lifting shop is a Star class 4-6-0, and a King Class 4-6-0. Standing outside the shed are a Dean Goods class 0-6-0 and a Saint Class 4-6-0. The building seen here was opened in 1894 and replaced an earlier wooden structure. It closed to steam on 14 October 1963.

Abercynon shed in the 1930s. The shed seen here was constructed in 1929 and replaced the original Taff Vale shed which stood on the same site. In view from right to left is Auto Fitted Metro Tank 2-4-0 no 3599, 5600 class 0-6-2TS no 5643 and 5637, and ex Taff Vale A class 0-6-2T no 357 together with other members of the class. Abercynon closed in November 1964.

One of the two roundhouses at Neath (Court Sart) on 2 June 1926. A locomotive shed was opened here in 1876. Amongst others (from L to R) are Dean Goods 0-6-0 no 2358, 0-6-0ST no 2175, and 0-6-0 PT nos 2085 and 1690.

The wooden shed at Oxford. The ancient wooden engine shed at Oxford dates from around 1863. For such a busy shed it was never rebuilt and remained in this condition until its closure to steam on 31 December 1965. It is pictured here in the 1930s with a 6300 class 2-6-0, a 455 class 2-4-0T, and a Hall class 4-6-0 waiting to leave the depot. The wagons seen behind the locomotive are part of a goods train passing by on the adjacent down line.

Leamington was a typical Churchward designed 4 road brick built shed. Opened in September 1906 it is seen here in around 1946 when it had an allocation of 32 locomotives and diesel railcars. On view are a 5100 class 2-6-2T, a 2900 Saint Class 4-6-0 and a 5600 class 0-6-2T. It was closed to steam on 14 June 1965.

One of the more interesting engine sheds was St Blazey. This 9 road brick built half roundhouse was constructed by the Cornwall Minerals Railway in 1872. It is pictured here in 1936 with a pair of 0-6-0 pannier tanks in view. At this time it had an allocation of 37 locomotives. Access to the shed roads was via a turntable. The shed was closed to steam in April 1962 and was for many years after used as a diesel stabling point. Today, the building is listed and is severed from the railway. It is currently in commercial use.

The small shed at Whitland taken in November 1938. The shed building seen here was moved from Letterston and erected at Whitland in 1902; it was rebuilt using corrugated iron shortly after this picture was taken. Whitland was a sub-shed of Neyland and closed in December 1963. On view are 4300 Class 2-6-0 no 7318 and a pair of 0-6-0PTs.

Sub sheds were a feature on the Great Western system. A typical example was Marlborough, seen here in May 1929. The single road shed was opened by the Marlborough Railway in April 1864, and closed in July 1933. Standing alongside the shed is Auto-fitted Metropolitan class 2-4-0T no 1499.

The small wooden shed at Pantrilas was sub shed to Pontypool Rd and was situated on the Pontypool to Hay-on-Wye branch. It is pictured here on 20 July 1935 with 5800 class 0-4-2T no 5818. It was closed on 2 February 1953.

Many of the larger sheds had their own repair shops; this is the one at Old Oak Common. It had twelve roads and was known locally as 'The Factory', served by an outside traverser. The 'factory' was opened together with the adjacent locomotive shed on 17 March 1906. In this 1947 view, the repair shop contains a King Class 4-6-0, two Castle Class 4-6-0s, one Hall class 4-6-0, two 6100 class 2-6-2Ts and a 5700 class 0-6-0PT. After Old Oak was closed to steam in March 1965, it continued in use as a diesel repair shop, and in later years it was used by the engineering department.

SWINDON LOCOMOTIVE WORKS

The Great Western opened its railway works at Swindon on 2 January 1843. Initially the works were used for the repair, and later the assembly of locomotives. It was not until April 1846 that the first locomotive to be completely built at Swindon was turned out. This was a 2-2-2 tender locomotive designed by Gooch, that was aptly named *Great Western*. From that date, the works expanded constantly from 14½ acres in 1848, to an area of 326 acres in 1947. The works eventually comprised three main sections, the Locomotive Department and the Carriage and Wagon departments. This constant expansion saw the number of employees increase from 4,500 in 1876 to its heyday in the 1920s and 1930s when the total reached nearly 14,000; even by the early 1950s the figure was around 10,000. In 1960, Swindon had the honour of constructing the last steam locomotive for British Railways, BR Standard 9F 2-10-0 no 92220 *Evening Star*. The removal of steam from the Western Region in 1965 saw the role of the works diminish. The

The interior of the old B shop at Swindon is seen here around the turn of the last century. This picture shows the vertical boiler steam powered traverser to good effect. In 1921 the capacity of the new 'A' shop was almost doubled, with the extended building covering an area of 11½ acres. In 1929, with its work switched to the enlarged 'A' shop, and in order to free up some more outside space the old B shop was demolished.

original carriage and wagon shops were sold and became a small business park. The last diesels were constructed in 1965 and although locomotive and DMU repairs continued the works became part of the British Rail Engineering Ltd. Deemed to be surplus to requirements the works were closed by BREL Ltd on 26 March 1986.

'A' shop was opened in 1901 and is pictured here in May 1904. In view amongst many others are 517 class 0-4-2T no 528 and no 552 and 0-6-0 ST no 1971.

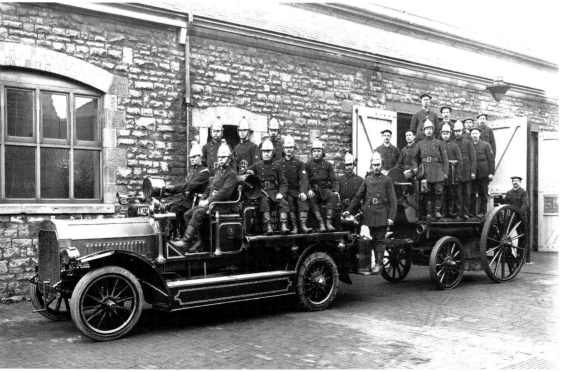

The men of the Swindon Works fire brigade pose for the camera in 1915. With the First World War in progress, many of those in the brass fire helmets appear to be middle aged or older.

The iron foundry at Swindon in 1925. At its peak, the foundry was producing between 9,000 and 10,000 tons of finished castings each year. This must have been both a dangerous and noisy place, but closer inspection shows a total lack of ear or eye protection for the men.

A locomotive test plant was built by Churchward in 'A' shop at Swindon in 1903, and was still in use some 60 years later. Pictured here standing on the test plant in around 1928 is Badminton Class 4-4-0 no 4113 *Samson*. The engine record sheet shows that no 4113 was in the works between January 1928 and July 1930, for 'demonstrations of the test plant for visitors to the works'.

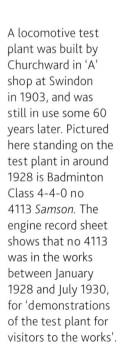

The interior of the Great Western Drawing office at Swindon. Plans were produced here for the largest locomotives, right down to the smallest screw.

What a wonderful place for the spotter, A shop at Swindon taken on 18 March 1925. In view amongst others are Star Class 4-6-0 4022 *King William* on the hoist, 4200 class 2-8-0T no 4221, and Saint Class 4-6-0 no 2909 *Lady of Provence*.

This rather humorous picture, taken in the works probably in 1927, illustrates the change in chimney design over the years. One assumes that there was no one inside the 1837 chimney.

The interior of A shop taken on 22 May 1936 shows three Collett 2251 class 0-6-0s no's 2276, 2277 and 2278 under construction.

Locomotives left A shop after repair via the electric powered locomotive traverser. In May 1933 King Class 4-6-0 no 6004 *King George III* leaves A shop after a heavy general repair.

A turn of the last century postcard showing staff leaving the Railway Works at Swindon.

Another early postcard showing the GWR hospital at Swindon. The building was originally built as the X1 Wiltshire Volunteer Rifle Corps armoury but was taken over and converted to the GWR hospital in December 1871. The hospital was endowed with £1,000 from Sir Daniel Gooch, a sum which was matched by a rise in the members' weekly contributions to the staff medical fund. The fund provided a complete medical service that included both dental and eye clinics, a casualty department and a doctors' surgery. Each year in July, the Works ran a series of day excursions for the staff and their families. The following two humorous postcards probably sum up the experience of the travellers.

Before the trip. On the table is a tub of Condy's Fluid, this was a disinfectant (soap) wash that was popular at the time. The day of the trip. Compare the entrance to the excursion with the next photo.

ANNUAL TRIP. 1906
HOOPER SWINDON.

A copy of a postcard showing the start of a works trip in July 1906. Passenger safety seems to be non-existent with people wandering all over the various lines.

SIGNALLING

When the line was opened between Paddington and Maidenhead on 4 June 1838, it was initially patrolled by Company 'policemen'. These policemen were expected to control the trains using hand signals and to do this the line was divided up into 'beats'. A year or so later, when the line was opened through to Twyford, the points and crossings on the railway were being controlled by Switchmen. Signals as such were not used on the Great Western until March 1840, when the line was opened through to Reading. The first fixed signal appears to have been installed at Reading, as Gooch's regulations for locomotives working trains to Reading on or after 30 March 1840 states, 'A signal ball will be seen at the entrance to Reading Station when the line is right for the train to go in. If the ball is not visible, the train must not pass it'. However, by 1841, the signal balls had been replaced by the newly introduced Brunel -designed Disc and Crossbar type signals.

The first mention of a signal works at Reading does not appear until around 1859. Prior to this date, both the permanent way and fixed signals were maintained by district contractors. It appears that the GWR took over the plant of one of these contractors who were based in Slough and set up their own separate repair works based at Caversham, Reading, under the control of Mr Thomas Blackall, the first manager of the works. Initially the work was undertaken by just a handful of men, but the works expanded with the construction of footbridges, cranes and permanent way equipment. The first semaphore signals to be built at Reading were erected between Paddington and Kensal Green in April 1865. In 1872, the first interlocking frame was constructed at Caversham and installed at Taplow and by this date the works had expanded to employ some 500 men. On 27 July 1903, the signalling and telegraph departments were amalgamated which resulted some 397 staff moving from Westbourne Park to Caversham. Between 1896 and 1910, the works were turning out some 150 signal boxes per year. Some idea of the amount of equipment produced by the signalling department can be gleaned from the 1923 *Great Western Magazine* which lists particulars of signal equipment in use at that time. This comprised 2,066 signal boxes, 23,467 signals, 58,680 working levers, 14,456 points, 4,824 facing points locking sets, 11,025 independent discs, 683 ground frames, 354 level crossing gates and 501 electrically worked signals. The signal works at Caversham was closed on 29 June 1984

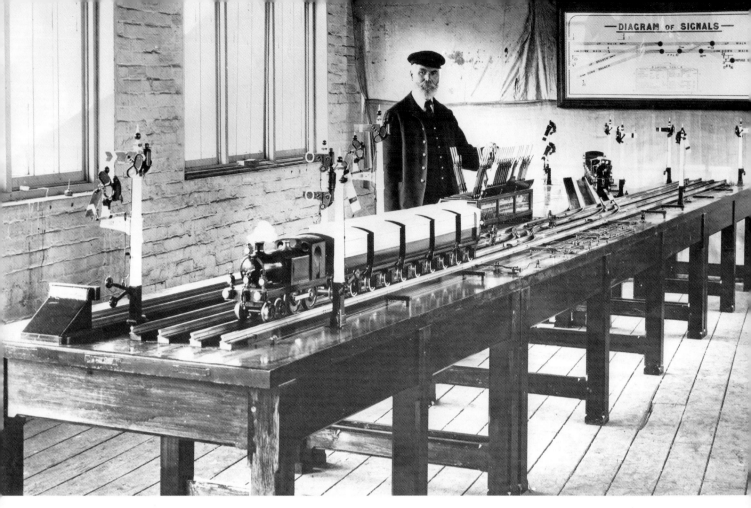

A wonderful picture of the original GWR signalling school at Caversham taken around the turn of the last century. Note the miniature frame controlling points and signals. The first interlocking frame on the Great Western was built at Caversham in 1872 for use at Marlow.

The wooden signal box at Maidenhead Bridge, probably taken shortly after the gauge conversion. This box stood just to the East of the bridge but had a rather short life, opening on 8 September 1884, and closing on June 1893.

The angular wooden Didcot East End Cabin taken in May 1892. The signal box was constructed in around 1874 and contained a 57 lever frame. It was closed on 23 October 1932.

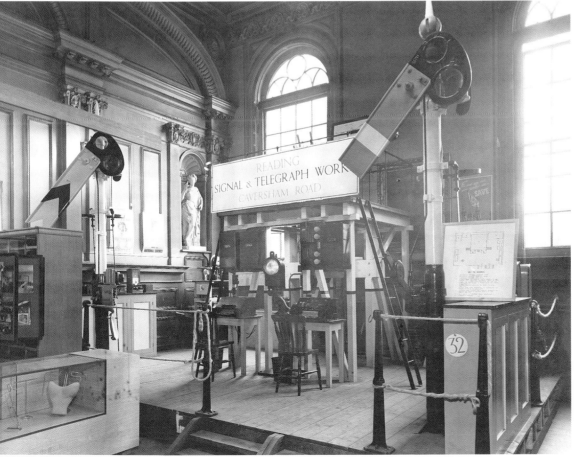

A display of signalling equipment constructed at Caversham Road seen here on display inside the Town Hall at Reading. The occasion was an exhibition of local trades, put on by the National Savings movement.

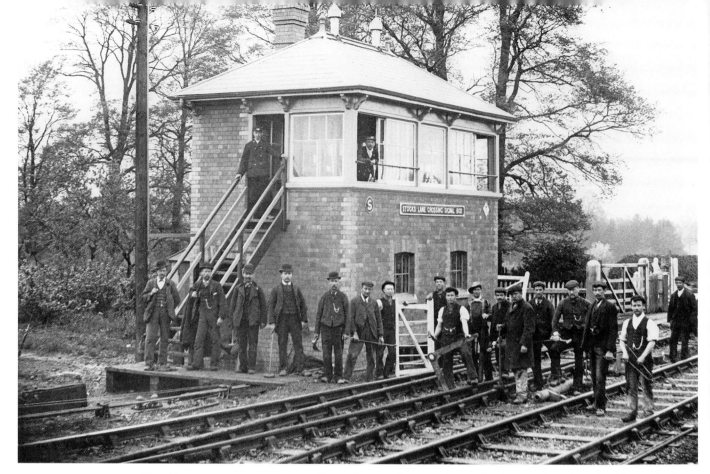

Signal box and permanent way staff pose for the photographer at Stocks Lane Crossing Signal Box, Newland near Worcester. Stocks Lane was fitted with a 21-lever frame and was opened in December 1899. It is seen here in probably soon after opening. Notice the circular S and triangle T (signal and telegraph) at each end of the box. It was renamed Newland East in 1929.

The interior of Friars Junction signal box taken on 2 August 1902. The box had a 71-lever frame and was opened on 9 March 1902 and closed on 8 October 1962.

Reading West Main signal box, seen here in November 1938. This box, a replacement for an earlier box, was opened in around 1896 and contained a 222-lever frame, the largest mechanically operated box on the Great Western and later Western Region. The frame was the largest to be constructed at the Caversham Road works and weighed some 100tons. The box was closed on 26 April 1965 with the opening of a new power box at Reading.

A view of Didcot East Junction signal box pictured here soon after it opened on 23 October 1932. The box which replaced an earlier box was constructed of concrete slabs and contained a 150-lever frame. A number of these concrete boxes were constructed at this time. The box was closed on 17 May 1965 when the new power box at Reading took control of Didcot.

ACCIDENTS

The Great Western generally ran a safe railway, but over the years there were many accidents, these were mainly collisions that were often caused by human error, or derailments caused by the state of the track.

Accidents of any sort invariably attract spectators. Today the public would not get near a railway accident, but in times past, things were different as some of following pictures show. Posing for the photographer seems to be the norm.

On 5 November 1868, the broad gauge Waverley Class 4-4-0 *Rob Roy*, hauling the 5pm up service from Milford comprising three coaches and a luggage van, ran at speed into the rear of a special goods and cattle train hauled by Caesar Class 0-6-0 *Tantalus* at Bullo Pill Junction some 12 miles south of Gloucester. Several passengers as well as a large number of cattle were killed.

The result of a head on collision at Norton Fitzwarren on 11 November 1890. In the foreground is a narrow gauge Standard Goods 0-6-0 no 1100 and behind an ex Bristol & Exeter 4-4-0ST no 2051. The 4-4-0ST was on an up special express service from Plymouth Millbay to London. Ten passengers were killed and many injured. No. 2051 was extensively damaged and immediately withdrawn, but no. 1100 was subsequently repaired and continued in service until being withdrawn in August 1916.

Dozens of spectators view the scene at Loughor near Llanelly on Monday 3 October 1904. An up express to London hauled by Atbara 4-4-0 no 3460 Montreal comprising eight coaches and a six wheeled van was being assisted up the bank to Cockett by an 0-6-0ST no 1674. Unfortunately, whilst travelling at about 25mph, the saddle tank which was at the front of the Atbara derailed and rolled onto its side, being hit by no 3460. A number of the wooden coaches were damaged, two quite badly. The driver of no. 1674 was killed together with two passengers; a further fifty were injured.

Old Oak Common allocated no 3710 *City of Bath* is pictured here at Yeovil Pen Mill on 8 August 1913 after colliding with the rear of a passenger train that was standing in the station, unfortunately killing two passengers. The following day, no 3710 was removed to Weymouth for repair, it obviously did not require a trip to Swindon and was returned to service on 7 October 1913.

An 850 class 0-6-0ST no 1905 in trouble after running through the wooden stop blocks and mounting the platform at Bodmin station on 19 June 1906. It was not badly damaged and was subsequently repaired at Newton Abbot. It had been built at Swindon in October 1881 and was converted to a pannier tank in December 1926 and was withdrawn from service in October 1936.

The result of a derailment at the entrance to Ledbury Tunnel on 11 April 1915. Aberdare Class 2-6-0 no 2604 from Cardiff on a Wolverhampton to Cardiff freight ran into a siding, demolishing the stop and turning over. There were no casualties, but the driver was trapped under the locomotive for some three hours before he could be released.

An accident at Aller Junction on 23 April 1929 when Hall Class 4-6-0 no 4909 Blakesley Hall on the 7.40 am service from Penzance ran into the back of the 5.50am goods service to Tiverton Junction. Thankfully there were only minor casualties.

Sometimes things just go wrong; in this undated view, a Rhymney Railway locomotive department breakdown crane will now need another crane to retrieve it after toppling over, and falling down an embankment near Cardiff. The accident happened whilst retrieving some derailed wagons.

PUBLICITY

ublicity was an important part of Great Western operations. During the early days, the advertising material comprised mainly black and white letterpress, but by the 1890s the Company had started to introduce colour. It is thought that the first colour pictorial poster, advertising Ascot races, was introduced in June 1897, and from around that date colour started to become the norm rather than the exception. One very successful aspect of the publicity department was the large amount of published material. By the 1920s and 1930s, the company was producing guide books, books for 'boys of all ages', jigsaws, and of course the wonderful double royal and quad royal posters. I have included the following illustrations to give an indication of the variation in advertising material produced by the Company. All of the items illustrated are from the extensive Great Western Trust publicity and poster collection.

A mock up of a Great Western Publicity stand seen here at Swindon on 14 July 1913 being prepared for display at the forthcoming Manchester Exhibition. Apart from the various posters, also on display is a Swindon apprentice model showing the workings of a Great Western 2-4-0.

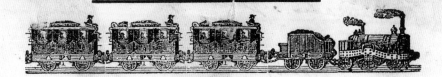

(No. 380.)

GREAT WESTERN RAILWAY.

EXCURSION

TO

LONDON

ON

MONDAY,

September 23rd, 1861,

an EXCURSION TRAIN will leave YEOVIL at 9.0 a.m.,

CALLING AS FOLLOWS:		A.M.	FARES:	
			FIRST CLASS.	CLOSED CAR.
Yeovil	at	9.0		
Sparkford	"	9.18		
Castle Carey	"	9.35	**11s**	**7s**
Bruton	"	9.45		
			FIRST CLASS.	CLOSED CAR.
Frome	at	10.10		
Westbury	"	10.25		
Trowbridge	"	10.40	**10s**	**6s**
Devizes	"	10.0		
Melksham	"	11.0		

and return from Paddington at **3.30 p.m.** on **Thursday,**
September 26th, 1861.

A single package of Luggage allowed each Passenger.

BRISTOL, 12th September, 1861.

ARROWSMITH, Time Tables' Office, Quay Street, Bristol.

Early advertising was accomplished by using simple and cheap letterpress sheets, with larger posters in the same style. This one dated 23 September 1861 is advertising an excursion from Yeovil to London. Notice the early illustration of a broad gauge train.

(No. 113.)

GREAT WESTERN RAILWAY.

NOTICE!

THE

GREAT EASTERN

STEAM SHIP

IS APPOINTED TO ARRIVE AT

WEYMOUTH

ON

FRIDAY, Sept. 9th,

and to remain there until the 16th or 17th.

The Public will be admitted on board until the evening of THURSDAY, the 15th inst.

FIRST and SECOND CLASS RETURN TICKETS at SINGLE FARES, available for the day only, will be issued at BRISTOL and intermediate Stations to YEOVIL inclusive, and also from SALISBURY and intermediate Stations to WESTBURY, commencing on the 9th and terminating on the 17th.

BRISTOL, Sept. 6th, 1859.

ARROWSMITH, Time Tables' Office, 11, Quay Street, Bristol.

Another letterpress sheet printed on red paper advertising tickets to see the arrival of Brunel's *Great Eastern* steamship on its maiden voyage from London to Weymouth on September 9 1859. Unfortunately for the travellers, the *Great Eastern* never made it to Weymouth on the 9th, due to an onboard explosion that occurred as the ship was in the channel near Hastings.

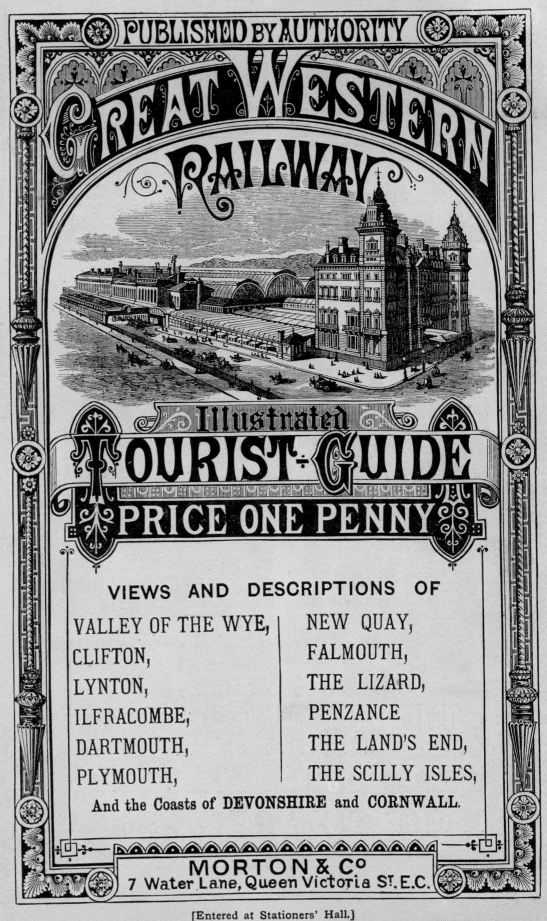

In the early days, guides to the Great Western Railway were published by private companies. This is a *Guide to the Great Western* (*Published by Authority*) in 1879 by Morton and Co.

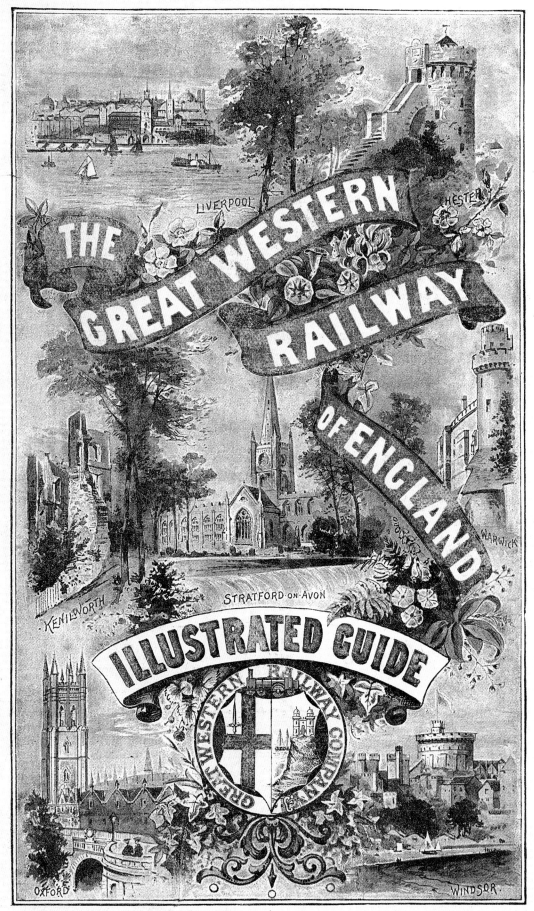

PADDINGTON STATION, *MARCH, 1895.*

An illustrated guide produced by the Great Western for overseas tourists visiting the country dated March 1895.

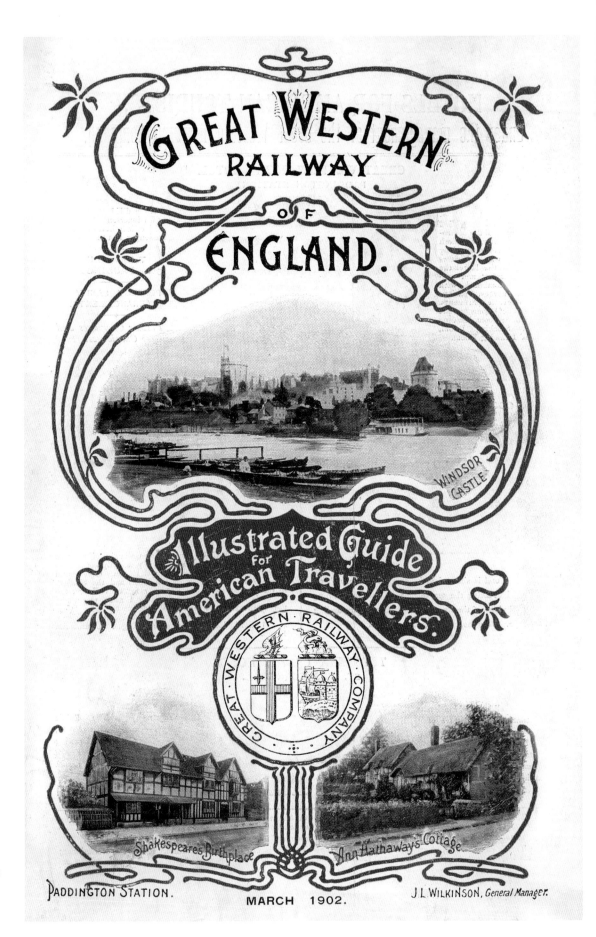

GREAT WESTERN
RAILWAY
OF
ENGLAND.

WINDSOR CASTLE

Illustrated Guide
for
American Travellers.

GREAT WESTERN RAILWAY COMPANY

Shakespeares Birthplace

Ann Hathaways Cottage

PADDINGTON STATION.

MARCH 1902.

J.L. WILKINSON, General Manager.

A similar guide this time aimed at the American traveller, March 1902.

CAMPING - HOLIDAYS

Published by the

GREAT WESTERN RAILWAY

Over the years, the company produced a number of specialist guide books such as *Camping Holidays 1925*.

Golf was a popular pastime, with the Great Western serving some of the top courses. This guide to golf courses on the GWR was published in 1925.

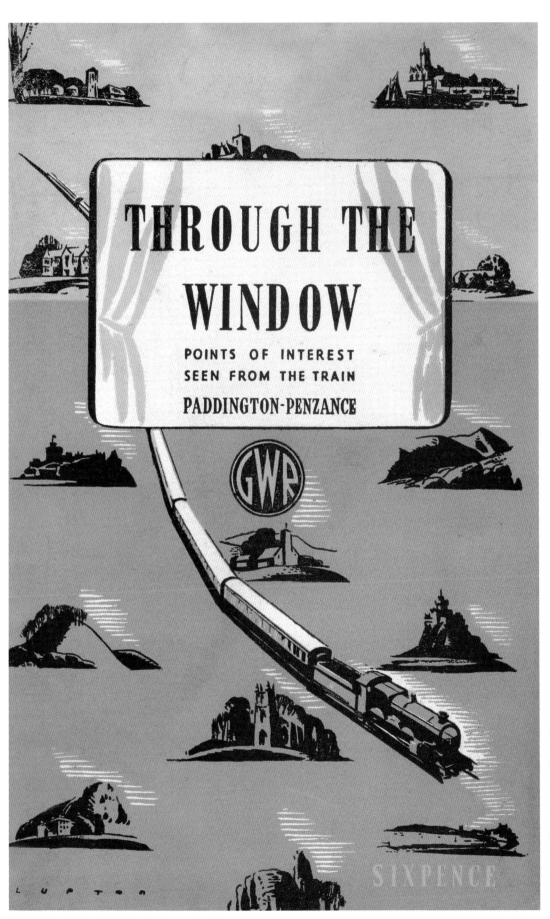

A popular publication was the *Through The Window* series. The guide described the journey and the highlights to be seen en route. This one is for the journey from Paddington to Penzance. These Through the Window guides were still being produced by the Western Region well into the 1960s.

The Great Western catered for the railway enthusiast with the publication of its engine books. The first *Names of Engines* book was published in 1911 and cost 6d, it was gradually enlarged over the years to include Names, Numbers, Types & Classes, together with illustrations of locomotives. This is the 1946 and last edition; the cover was designed by Charles Mayo, and the price has now increased to 2/6d. Contrary to the titles, none of the engine books gave a complete list of engine numbers; it would be left to a young lad called Ian Allan to provide those.

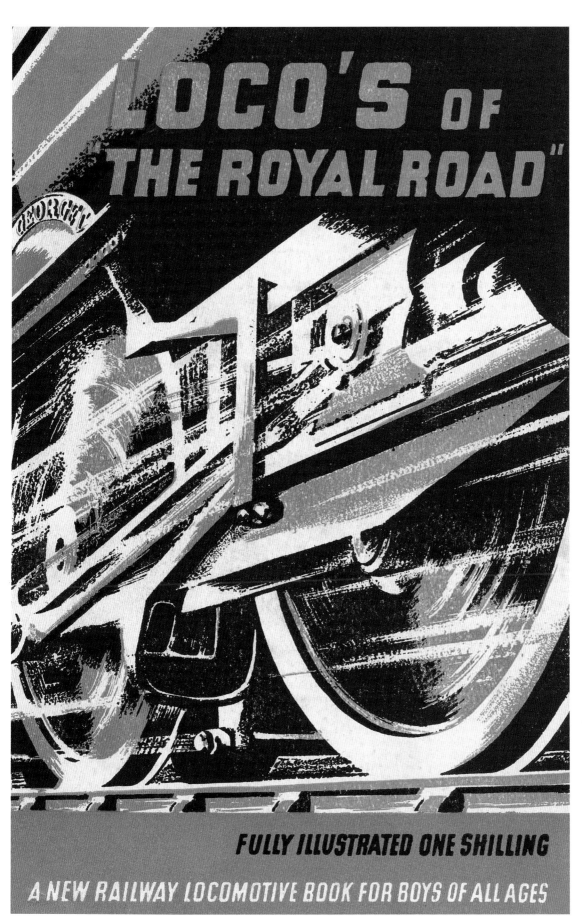

LOCO'S OF THE ROYAL ROAD"

GEORGE V

FULLY ILLUSTRATED ONE SHILLING

A NEW RAILWAY LOCOMOTIVE BOOK FOR BOYS OF ALL AGES

Locos of the Royal Road was a railway book for 'boys of all ages'. The company could have used the term 'enthusiasts of all ages' but 'boys of all ages' has a much better ring about it. The Company were very successful in marketing books for the railway enthusiast.

From 1924, the Great Western produced a large number of Jigsaw puzzles. These were priced at 2/6d and produced for the Company by the Chad Valley Company. The 150-piece Warwick Castle by the artist Warwick Doble dates from around 1930.

Brasenose College Oxford was produced from 1933 and contained about 400 pieces. It was initially priced at 5 shillings but with poor sales it was soon reduced to the standard charge of 2s 6d. Notice the use of the word 'about' when specifying the number of pieces; this was because the puzzles were cut by hand.

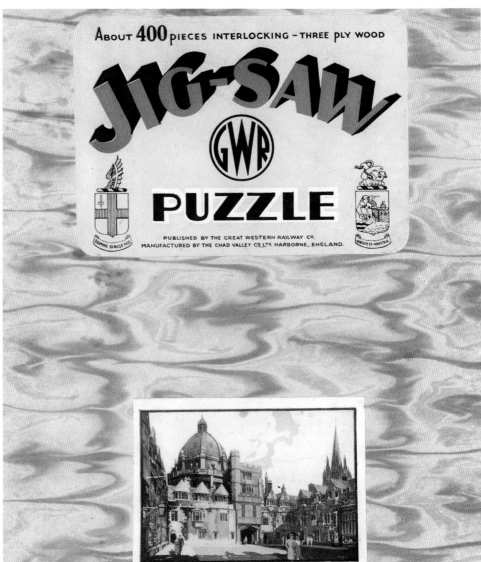

Postcards were produced for sale by the Great Western Publicity Department from around 1903. Many of these images were facsimiles of the larger posters that could be seen around the system.

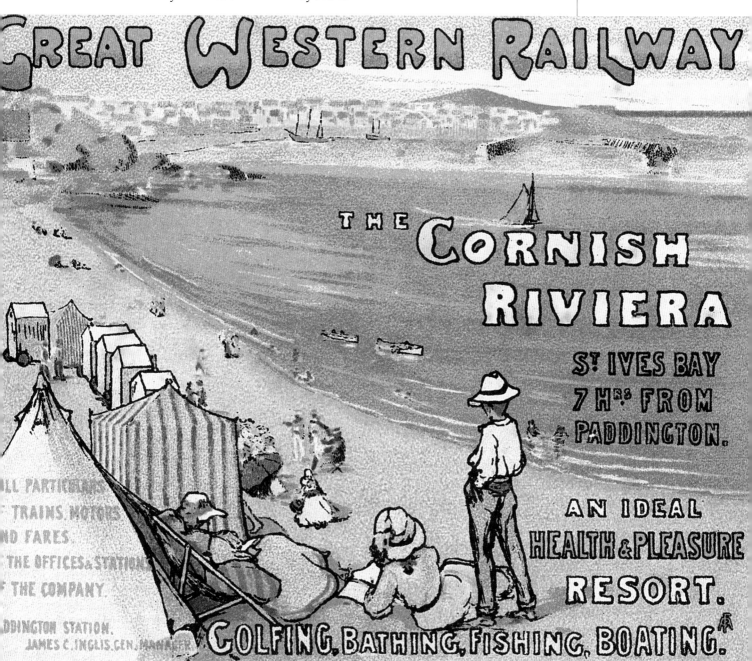

A postcard advertising the Cornish Riviera, c 1903.

Xmas Excursions November 1903 by the artist George Conning.

GREAT WESTERN RAILWAY

PICTURESQUE WALES

Tourist Tickets

CHEAP EXCURSIONS
DURING
SUMMER

FROM LONDON
AND ALL
PRINCIPAL STATIONS.

TENBY

JAMES C. INGLIS, General Manager

Picturesque Wales
c 1905.

The upper Thames
c 1905.

Another poster facsimile advertising weekend tickets circa 1904. by the artist William Tompkin.

1930 guide to Holidays on the Great Western, cover illustration by D Penty. These free guides to 'The Ideal Holiday Lands of the Great Western' were published annually during the period between the wars. This one contains 60 pages with each holiday area described and illustrated with black and white photos, unlike Holiday Haunts the Holiday Guides contain no commercial advertising.

WINTER
has no discomforts in
CORNWALL

Where there is a Maximum of Warmth & Comfort

IN Sunny Cornwall winter has no rigours ; hail and frost are practically unknown, snow seldom falls. The climate is marvellously mild and equable—as mild as, and more equable than, the southern winter resorts on the Continent. Spend a winter holiday in the Cornish Riviera — the land where winter is almost as gentle as June.

THESE METEOROLOGICAL TEMPERATURE CHARTS SHOW THE WONDERFUL DIFFERENCE OF THE CORNISH WINTER CLIMATE FROM THAT OF LONDON.

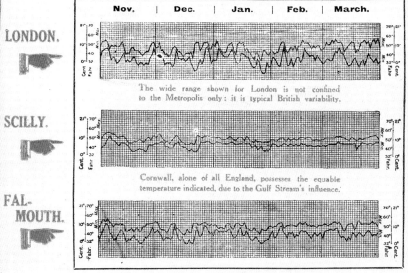

Fast Express Services from all parts by comfortable trains.
Ask at Stations for details of Week-End and Tourist Fares.

G.W.R.—The Winter Holiday Line.
FRANK POTTER, General Manager.

The Winter Line, encouraging the traveller to the joys of a winter holiday in the south west, by comparing temperatures in London, Falmouth and the Scilly Islands. c 1914.

St Ives and Carbis Bay 1935 with the new GWR roundel. By this date, the posters were much simpler in style and featured the work of top artists of the day, in this case, Herbert Truman.

LONDON PRIDE

One of my favourite posters is London Pride by the artist Frank Mason. It was produced in 1946 and the simple title probably sums up the thoughts of many Londoners at this time. Noel Coward composed his famous song *London Pride* during the blitz in spring 1941. He apparently got the idea whilst sitting waiting for a train at Paddington and seeing everyone 'just getting on with life'.

An important publication that was produced annually by the publicity department was the famous *Holiday Haunts* guide. This publication contained details of all of the resorts situated on the Great Western together with suitable hotels and guest houses. It was first published in 1906 and was still being produced in a slightly different guise after nationalisation by the Western Region. A feature of the later publications were the front covers many featuring bathing belles.

The precursor of the *Holiday Haunts* was published by Walter Hill; this is the cover the 1899 edition. This guide proved to be very popular, and in 1906, the Great Western publicity Department produced its own version, naming it *Holiday Haunts*.

The 1906 first edition of *Holiday Haunts* was produced with a blue and grey cover, it contained 334 pages and was priced at 1d. The early editions had a separate section for Southern Ireland which at this time was still part of the UK.

HOLIDAY HAUNTS
1929

From 1911 to 1928, *Holiday Haunts* was produced with a plain buff cover, but the 1929 edition was the first to be produced with a colour illustration on the cover. It contained 976 pages and was priced at 6d. The bathing beauty was to be a cover feature on many of the subsequent editions.

The 1931 edition
it comprised 978
pages and was
edited by Maxwell
Fraser. It features
an attractive young
bather by the artist
D. Penty on the
cover. It is recorded
as having a print run
of around 200,000
copies.

HOLIDAY HAUNTS

1935

SIXPENCE

GWR

CENTENARY NUMBER

The 1935 *Centenary Edition* surprisingly had a rather dull cover in chocolate and cream but now featured the new GWR roundel. It had expanded to an amazing 1024 pages.

The 1939 edition contains 968 pages. The cover has a family friendly illustration of two young holidaymakers by the artist Muriel Gill.

Holiday Haunts 1947

GWR

SIXPENCE

FRANK SOAR

The 1947 edition was the 32nd and the last Great Western edition. It was still priced at 6d but now contained just 688 pages. The rather racy cover illustration by the artist Frank Soar probably reflects the post war optimism.

NAMED TRAINS

The Great Western was well known for its many named trains, probably the most famous of these was the 'Cornish Riviera Express'. What is interesting is that well after nationalisation in 1948, the newly formed Western Region actively expanded the number of 'named trains' on its system, the 1959 timetable contains sixteen 'named trains' plus two other inter-regional 'named' services, and even today the tradition continues with the 10.06 HST service from Paddington to Penzance and the 08.44 up service still being announced as the 'Cornish Riviera Express'.

G. W. R. Flying Dutchman

Between 1862 and 1904, the principal service between Paddington and Cornwall was known as 'The Flying Dutchman', a named derived from the winner of both the Derby and St Ledger races in 1849. For many years the 'Dutchman' held the distinction of being the fastest train in the country, running between Paddington and Plymouth (via Bristol) in just 6¼ hours. The removal of the broad gauge in May 1892 saw the 'Dutchman' service gradually downgraded, although in 1906 and now running via Westbury, for a short time it was speeded up to reach Plymouth in 5½ hours, eventually being eclipsed by the much faster 'Cornish Riviera Express' service. This postcard view shows 'The Flying Dutchman 'service near Goring hauled by a Dean Single 3031 class 4-2-2.

The Great Western's flagship service was the 'Cornish Riviera Express'. The service essentially started on 1 July 1904 with the introduction of the first regular non-stop run between Paddington and Plymouth. Known as the 'Limited', it initially it ran during the summer months only but from 1906 with the opening of the direct route via Westbury and Castle Cary it ran all year round. The service left Paddington at 10.10am, but in July 1906, the departure time was altered to 10.30 am with the journey time to Plymouth cut to just 4hr 25 minutes, before eventually arriving at Penzance at 5.10pm. The name, it seems, came from the public who were invited via the 1904 railway magazine to submit a name for the new service. Two stood out, 'Cornish Riviera Limited' and 'Royal Duchy Express'. Mr J.C. Inglis, the General manager at the time, selected 'Riviera Express'. The prefix Cornish was soon being used and the service became known as 'Cornish Riviera Limited Express'. However for many years it was known by the staff as 'The Limited'. The up 'Riviera' comprising 'Centenary' stock is pictured here near Somerton on 20 August 1935 hauled by King Class 4-6-0 no 6023 King Edward II. These superb coaches were introduced on this service in 1935 to celebrate the centenary of the Great Western Railway.

The down service hauled by an almost brand new King Class 4-6-0 no 6004 King George III makes a fine sight as it passes a pair of young enthusiasts at Twyford (Bucks) in August 1927.

The Great Western's first and only Pullman service was the 'Torquay Pullman'. Comprising six Pullman cars, is seen here hauled by a King class 4-6-0 no 6015 *King Richard III*. The service was introduced during the summer of 1929 but was not successful and was subsequently withdrawn at the end of the 1930 season. In the 1950s, the Western Region introduced its rather more successful 'South Wales Pullman' business service.

A great shot of Star Class 4-6-0 no 4070 *Neath Abbey* passing Twyford at speed on the 'Torbay Express' in the early 1930s. This service operated between Paddington and Kingswear, and at this time ran non-stop from Paddington to Exeter.

King Class 4-6-0 no 6029 *King Edward VIII* is pictured here hauling the 7 coach 'Bristolian' non-stop service, probably soon after its inauguration on 9 September 1935. The down service left Paddington at 10am with the up service departing Bristol at 4.30pm; both up and down services had booked times of 105 minutes.

For many years, the Great Western's 'Cheltenham Spa Express' service held the record for the fastest regular railway service in the world. The service which soon became known as the 'Cheltenham Flyer' was inaugurated in 1923, and over the years was gradually speeded up. The heyday of the 'Flyer' was probably in the 1930s when in September 1932, the schedule for the 77.3 miles from Swindon to Paddington was cut to just 65 minutes, which required a start to stop average of 71.4 mph. The fastest recorded up run took place on 6 June 1932, with Castle Class 4-6-0 no 5006 *Tregenna Castle*, covering the 77.3 miles in just 56 minutes and 47 seconds, an average speed of 81.7 mph. On the same day, the 5pm down service hauled by fellow Castle no.5005 *Manorbier Castle,* covered the distance in 60 min and 1 sec. The 7 coach up service is pictured here east of Swindon in around 1936 hauled by Castle Class no 5043 *Barbury Castle* (renamed *Earl of Mount Edgecumbe* in September 1937).

An opportunity to travel at a cheap fare
BY
"THE CHELTENHAM FLYER"
THE FASTEST TRAIN IN THE WORLD
(77¼ Miles in 65 Minutes SWINDON TO PADDINGTON)
Average Speed 71.35 Miles per hour.

EACH WEEKDAY
WEDNESDAYS, MARCH 1st, to APRIL 12th, inclusive,
HALF-DAY EXCURSION BOOKINGS
WILL BE GIVEN TO
SWINDON
AS UNDER:—
PADDINGTON .. dep. 1.18 p.m.
SWINDON .. arr. 3. 2 p.m.
(LUNCHEON CAR TRAIN.)

RETURN BY "THE CHELTENHAM FLYER"
(The Fastest Train in the World.)

				Distance from Swindon	
				Miles.	Chains.
SWINDON	..	..	.. dep. 3.50 p.m.	—	—
Didcot	..	..	.. pass 4.11 p.m.	24	14
Reading ..	..	..	.. „ 4.24 p.m.	41	26
Slough ..	..	..	„ 4.37 p.m.	58	68
Southall	..	..	„ 4.44½ p.m.	68	18
PADDINGTON	..	..	.. arr. 4.55 p.m.	77	24

RETURN FARES
FIRST CLASS
8/6
THIRD CLASS
5/0

☞ **The number of tickets issued each day will be strictly limited and application should be made in advance to the Booking Office at Paddington Station.**

This advertising bill dated February 1933 offered the general public a chance to ride from Swindon to Paddington on the famous 'Cheltenham Flyer'.

GOODS SERVICES

Goods services have always formed an important part of railway operations in this country. From the earliest days of the railway, the revenue from goods traffic was eclipsed by passenger traffic, but as goods services increased so did the revenue, and from around 1852 the revenue from goods services started to overtake that of passenger services. This increase continued and between 1865 and 1965 the difference in revenue between passenger and goods traffic was some 30% to 50% higher. From the early 1950s onwards, the increase in the use of road transport to move goods both locally and around the country saw the amount of goods carried on the railways decline.

Goods trains were introduced on the Great Western soon after the line was opened through to Twyford in September 1839. From the opening, the Great Western had been operating a nightly coke train from Paddington to Twyford and it is on this train that the first goods were carried. From these early beginnings, and as the system extended, so did the goods services. The trains were generally slow and short, but the expansion of the standard gauge from 1872 brought a subsequent increase in traffic. In 1842, goods receipts totalled £26,845, but by 1870, the revenue from goods traffic had increased to £2,218,998 which represented 52% of the company's annual turnover. The end of the broad gauge saw the introduction of more powerful locomotives which enabled goods services to be increased in length and weight. The introduction of the vacuum brake also saw the introduction of faster 'fully-fitted' vacuum brake services, but even with these faster services, the slow and time consuming pick up goods trains continued right through to the mass closure of many of the branch lines during 1960s.

Horse Power

From the early days of the Great Western, horses formed an important part in the operation of the Company's goods services, and by the turn of the last century the Great Western were using around 3,000 horses for both delivery and shunting duties.

In 1884, the Great Western established its Horse Provender Store at Didcot. This was the chief fodder store for the horses used by the company. Records show that in October 1906 the weekly quantities required were 1000 sacks of oats, 220 sacks of beans, 480 sacks of maize, 110 tons of hay, 16 tons of oat straw, 18 tons of bran and 40-50 tons of straw. The mixture for country horses was-oats 22½%, beans 10%, maize 20%, hay 41½%, and oat straw 6%. London horses were supplied with 2½% more oats and a slightly lower amount of hay. The Provender Store is pictured here around 1926.The wagon loads of hay can be seen in the yard. In the foreground is Didcot allocated 302 class 0-6-0ST number 307 together with a shunters truck. Over the years, the Didcot based 0-6-0s that were used to shunt the provender store yard were for obvious reasons fitted with spark arrestor chimney's.

The station staff together with the station shunting horse pose for the photographer at Wantage Road Station probably soon after the removal of the broad gauge. Many stations had their own horses for both shunting and delivery purposes.

In 1890 there were some 1100 horses in London alone. Pictured here in August 1925, together with his attendant, is the last shunting horse to be used at Paddington High Level yard. These working horses were particularly well looked after.

This slightly faded picture shows one of Reading's horses on station shunting duty. It is being used to move an early slip coach that had previously been slipped from the up 'Flying Dutchman' service at Reading station. The slip coach seen here was one of eighteen built in 1889 and numbered in the 7020-7038 series.

Witney blankets loaded ready for to delivery to Maples at Paddington goods circa 1910. The blankets would have been transported by rail from Witney, Oxfordshire to Paddington. Notice that the third team of Paddington horses appear to be greys. There were two major manufacturers of Witney blankets at this time, James Marriott and Sons and Charles Early and Co. Both companies can trace their origins back to the 1600s. The increasing popularity of the duvet brought about a decline in the popularity of blankets and in 1960, with a sharp fall in sales, the two companies merged. Sadly, after a number of takeovers, in 2002 blanket manufacturing ceased at Witney when production moved to Derbyshire.

The Great Western goods depot at South Lambeth was opened for goods in full wagons on 5 December 1910 and was the only Great Western goods depot south of the Thames. It was constructed on the site of the Southwark and Vauxhall Waterworks and stood between the river Thames and Stewarts Lane Junction. Here, members of the goods staff together with their delivery horses pose for the camera in 1911. The depot was transferred to the Southern Region in 1968 and closed in November 1980. Notice what I assume to be electric lamps that can be lowered via pulleys.

Petrol Power

By the early 1920s, the Great Western were operating a large number of country lorry services. No 1936 an Associated Daimler lorry is pictured here at Woodhay on 24 September 1929 whilst on one such service. Notice the oil lamps, solid tyres and the cast GWR on the front of the vehicle.

Another country lorry service pictured here collecting milk from Wayside Farm Shrivenham on 2 October 1929. The vehicle is Associated Daimler no 1910.

Moving cars by rail, here an Austin 6 from the Austin Motor Works at Longbridge near Birmingham is being unloaded from a 10 ton Asmo van on 8 May 1930. Today a vast number of new motor vehicles are moved by rail on a daily basis, to and from docks situated around the country.

A typical branch line pick up goods service from the Launceston branch approaches Marsh Mills yard Plymouth on 7 May 1936, hauled by 2021 class 0-6-0PT no. 2116. Pick up goods services were a feature on many branch lines.

For many years, moving coal and anthracite was an important part of Great Western operations, with millions of tons per year being moved around the system. Pictured are the coal sidings at Swansea Docks in the 1920s, full of private owners' coal and anthracite wagons.

A long coal train from South Wales to London climbs up the bank from the Severn Tunnel at Patchway hauled by 2800 class 2-8-0 no 2810.

Farm moves were also an important part of railway services throughout the country. Often the farm move would entail the service travelling from one end of the country to another. This is well illustrated in the British Transport film collection which documents one such move from North Yorkshire to Sussex. Here, two Great Western delivery vehicles are loaded with poultry including chickens and ducks during one such farm move. Pictured here at Llanwrda, West Wales, on 2 October 1934.

Another farm move on 30 September 1947, as horses are loaded into wagons in preparation for a farm move from Llantarnam on the Great Western to West Grinstead on the Southern Railway. Notice the Border Collie keeping watch on the proceedings.

Seasonal vegetables were moved extensively on Great Western goods services. The services were usually fully fitted and designated as 'fast perishables'. One of these was Cornish Broccoli which was for many years was transported from Cornwall by rail. The many 'Broccoli' specials were a feature of the Broccoli season. In 1946, some 65,000 tons were conveyed, but increased competition from foreign growers saw a continued growth in Broccoli imported from Europe. Broccoli from Brittany is being loaded into 5 plank open wagons at Weymouth Quay in 1947. In the background is a Channel Islands boat train hauled by a 1361 class 0-6-0PT.

The goods must get through, pictured here during the big freeze up of winter 1947, 30 men from the Royal Naval Barracks Plymouth were seconded to the Great Western to help clear the Princetown Branch. They are seen here on a very cold 10 February 1947, clearing the snow at Peak Hill cutting. The severe weather cut off many communities for days and sometimes weeks.

The result of their action is seen here on 21 February 1947. Mrs M. Mead and family had trekked 1½ miles from their home at Hill Cottages Princetown to the station at King Tor where they were handed bread and other provisions. At this time the line was still blocked between King Tor and Princetown. The guards van is a long way from home.

STAFF

For many years, the railways in this country were one of the largest employers, it is often said that every family in the country probably had a relative that worked or had worked on the railway. The Great Western alone required thousands of staff to operate its services. It looked after its staff and actively encouraged them to partake in many sporting and cultural activities which catered for almost every interest The following selection of photographs illustrate some of these activities as well as the many jobs required to run the railway.

Great Western Railway St John's Ambulance crew pictured here during a fund raising day at Hereford in 1907.The Great Western were active promoters of first aid, with teams being formed at many of the larger stations and depots. Each year prizes were presented for the most outstanding teams.

A humorous look at First Aid training published in the 1935 *Great Western Magazine* entitled 'An ambulance man does his homework'.

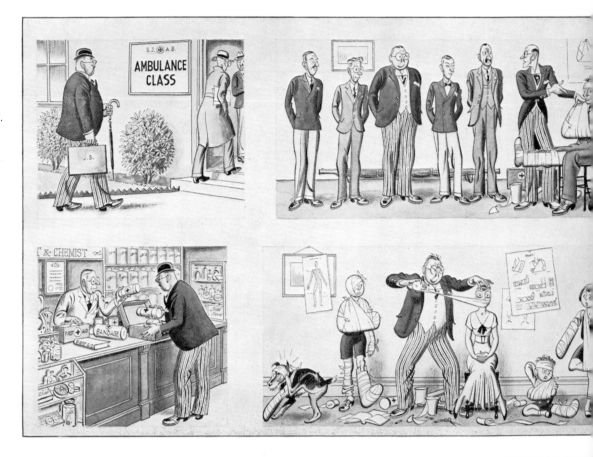

The Great Western operated a station gardens competition, with prizes being given for the best kept garden. The idea was of course to ensure that the stations were both clean and tidy and attractive to the traveller, many of whom wrote to the Company in appreciation of this. Here is the garden at Taplow being tended by members of the station staff.

Winners and runners up were presented with a certificate, and a cash prize to be shared amongst the station staff. This certificate shows that in 1927-30, Theale was awarded a second class prize of £3.00. Notice the change in General Manager on the award from Felix Pole to James Milne.

Sport played a big part in staff activities, with many of the sections and departments having their own sports teams. This picture shows the Oxford locomotive football team season 1910/11 pictured here with 3031 class 4-2-2 no 3053 *Sir Francis Drake*. The team played in the Oxford Senior league for many years. Many of the players seen here would have seen service during the First World War.

The Great Western Musical Society was another important pastime for staff that was actively supported by the Company. Its Chairman and President was for many years Sir Ernest Palmer, a Director of the Company. The Musical Society were very popular and gave concerts nationwide; this programme is rather nicely illustrated with drawings of Paddington and Swindon and is for a concert at the Queen's Hall in London on 16 February 1921. Queens Hall was an important London Concert Hall, opened in November 1893, and was unfortunately destroyed by an incendiary bomb on 10 May 1941. It never reopened.

Great Western Railway Concert

Wednesday, February 16th, 1921, 7.30 p.m.

Queen's Hall, Langham Place, W.1. (Oxford Circus Tube.)

Chairman and President, G. W. R. Musical Society: Sir S. Ernest Palmer, Bart.

Staff at Work

The top men on the operating side were the Drivers and Firemen as shown in this obviously posed shot of the crew in the cab of an unidentified Churchward locomotive.

The locomotive cleaning staff at Oxford in June 1912 with 3201 class 2-4-0 no 3207, an Oxford locomotive at this time. Most Drivers were very strict regarding the cleanliness of their locomotives. Many of these young lads would progress through the ranks to become Drivers and Firemen themselves.

Oiling up at Old
Oak Common
on 29 June 1934.
Castle Class no
5019 *Treago Castle*.

Ticket office staff at Paddington 1935. I wonder if the lady is also purchasing a ticket for the dog.

A wonderful picture of the mobile refreshment trolley attendant serving a customer at Paddington in 1935. Mobile refreshment trolleys were a feature on many of the larger stations for many years.

The following posed images were taken by photographer H White and show staff at work.

Chargeman Lenney pictured here turning a locomotive at Ranelagh Bridge, Paddington.

Fireman Alwyn at Wolverhampton Stafford Road.

Passenger shunter Courtney at Reading General.

Unnamed Carriage cleaners at Swindon.

The *Great Western Magazine*

The *Great Western Railway Magazine and Temperance Union Record* was the official staff magazine for Great Western employees. It was published monthly from 1862 until nationalisation in December 1947, after which it became the *British Railways Western Region Magazine*. From November 1890, 'Temperance Union Record' was dropped from the title, and from that date it became simply the *Great Western Railway Magazine*. The new *Magazine* was reduced in size but now

included photographic reproductions, and much more information regarding staff and railway operations. It was for many years offered in two editions, ordinary or art, the latter being printed on gloss paper which produced a higher quality image for the many photographs now being used. It was an important publication, being purchased by both the staff and the public alike. The information contained within its pages provides a social history of the Great Western. Some of the more interesting early covers are seen here.

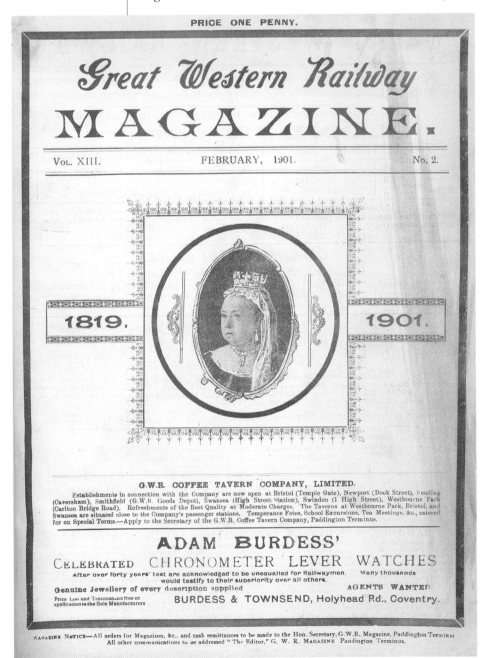

The February 1901 cover in purple commemorating the death of Queen Victoria. Interestingly, the cover also advertises the newly formed Great Western Railway Coffee Tavern Company. Coffee drinking was a popular pastime in years gone by as now, and Coffee Taverns were constructed on many stations.

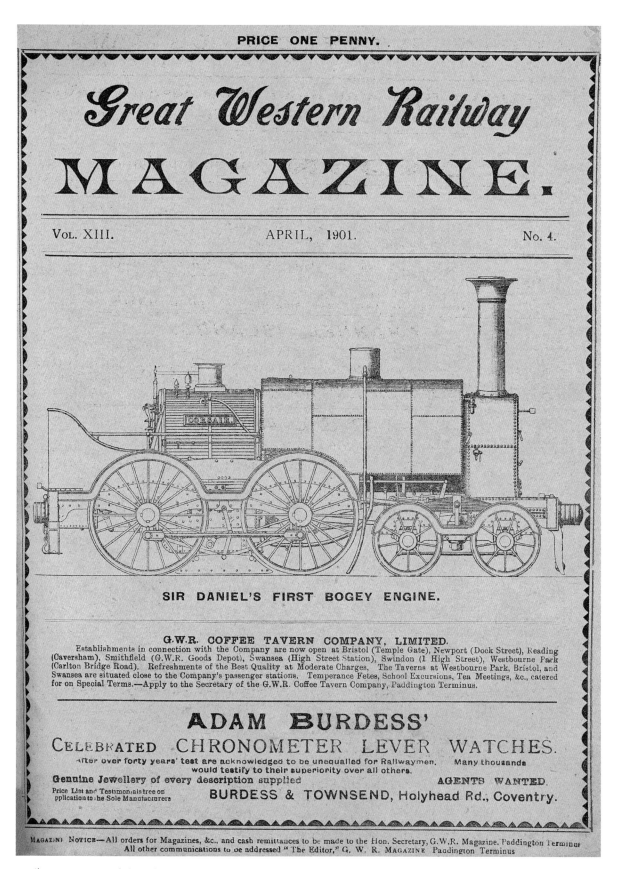

April 1901 cover with line diagram of Broad Gauge locomotive *Corsair*. *Corsair* was built at Swindon in August 1849, and withdrawn in June 1873, being subsequently sold for further use to the Cilely Colliery. Notice the early spelling of the word bogey.

The illustrated cover of the January 1907 edition with an illustration showing the Company Crest, a train and a ship. The cover also promoted the Ordinary edition of the magazine at 1d or Art 'white cover' edition 2d.

GREAT WESTERN RAILWAY
MAGAZINE

DECEMBER · 1947   VOL. 59 · NO. 11

PRIDE IN THE JOB
Sir James Milne, K.C.V.O., C.S.I., General Manager, Great Western Railway, 1929—1947

PRICE ONE PENNY

December 1947, the last Great Western edition published with plain black and white paper cover and featuring Sir James Milne, the last general manager of the Great Western Railway, who had just announced his retirement. The magazine contained a statement from the Chairman Viscount Portal to all employees regarding the forthcoming Nationalisation of the Company. Notice that it is still priced at 1d.

MOTOR BUS SERVICES

The first Road Motor bus services operated by the Great Western were inaugurated between Helston and the Lizard on Monday 17 August 1903. On 31 October of the same year, another new service was introduced between Penzance and Marazion. The bus services were gradually extended to cover many areas of the system including Cornwall, Devon, Somerset, South Wales, the Midlands and the Home Counties.

By the 1920s, the Great Western were operating what was probably the largest bus fleet in the country. This essentially came to an end with the passing in 1928 of the Great Western Railway (Road Transport)Act, which eventually led to the services being transferred from the Great Western to private bus companies, the result being that by 1934 all GWR motor bus services were being operated by other bus companies.

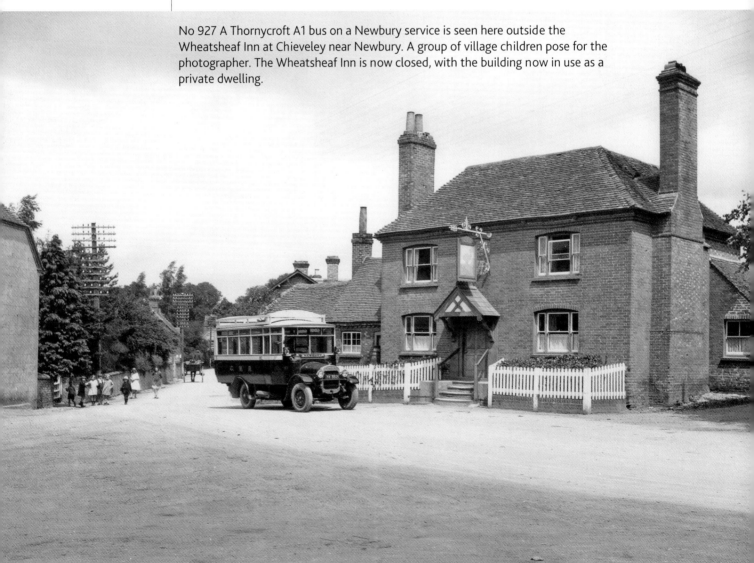

No 927 A Thornycroft A1 bus on a Newbury service is seen here outside the Wheatsheaf Inn at Chieveley near Newbury. A group of village children pose for the photographer. The Wheatsheaf Inn is now closed, with the building now in use as a private dwelling.

Passengers and crew of road motor no. 8 pose for the camera at Helston in Cornwall. One wonders whether the lady passenger feels safer sitting with the driver than in the back with the men!!

A bit of a prang. Great Western no 38, a 20hp Wolseley, chassis no A27, is pictured here in July 1905 after colliding with a tree in Mackenzie Street, Slough. No 38 (BHO4) was registered in Buckinghamshire and entered traffic on 3 April 1905; it was probably withdrawn after the accident.

No less than three GWR Thornycroft A1 road motors are in view as crowds arrive for a race meeting at Newbury Racecourse.

Dozens of Great Western road motor vehicles of different shapes and sizes parked up at Ascot in around 1912.

A postcard showing a GWR bus on the service from Plymouth to Tamerton Foliot seen here at the terminus at Tamerton Foliot. Note the solid tyres, not a comfortable ride one would imagine.

A Great Western bus stands outside the Tregenna Castle Hotel in St Ives, probably during the early 1920s. A GWR bus was stationed here for many years to take customers to and from the nearby St Ives Station. The hotel itself was built as a private dwelling in 1774, it was leased to the GWR in around 1878 and purchased outright by the Company in 1895, becoming one the GWR's principal hotels. It eventually became part of the British Transport Hotels group but was sold off in 1980. Today it is still a top hotel.

CAMP COACHES

For many years the Great Western promoted 'Camp Coaches' as an inexpensive and great way to enjoy a rural or seaside holiday. These coaches had previously been withdrawn from regular passenger service and during the summer of 1933 some nineteen were converted at Swindon into camp coaches. The coaches were then placed around the system in preparation for the 1934 season. They were sited in station sidings and yards, either near the sea, or in areas of outstanding natural beauty. They were extensively advertised by the Great Western for use by railway employees and the public alike. The coaches became very popular, and for the 1936 season, the Great Western had a camp coach in no less than 50 different locations, and by 1939 this number had risen to 65. Interestingly, as the coaches were placed at or near stations, a discount was given on the hire of the coaches if the occupants travelled by train. One of these camp coaches survives at Didcot Railway Centre. The coach, no 416, was built by Dean in 1891 as a four wheeled brake 3rd. Diagram T39 lot no 582 and was converted into a camp coach no.9940 in 1933. At Didcot, it has been converted back into a brake 3rd, but it still retains the bunk beds in the guard's van.

What a wonderful tranquil setting, Camp Coach type C no 9953 in the station siding at Gara Bridge on the Kingsbridge branch 1934. This coach was built as Lavatory 1st/2nd class combo in 1892 on Lot 591. It was numbered 370 and after the 1907 renumbering 7370. The 21 on end is the weight in tons of the coach in running order.

1934 Pamphlet advertising the new Camp Coach holidays as 'novel and inexpensive'.

Camp Coach type C no 9984 on the Barmouth to Pwllheli line at Duffryn on Sea July 1934. This was built as a six wheeled tri-compo with a luggage compartment in 1884 on Lot 286 being numbered 244, and then 6244 after the 1909 renumbering scheme.

Camp Coach type C no 9982 stands in the siding at Barmouth Junction in 1935. Occupants of this coach had a wonderful view of the Estuary and mountains.

A small kitchen was provided, but looking at the churns, not it seems running water.

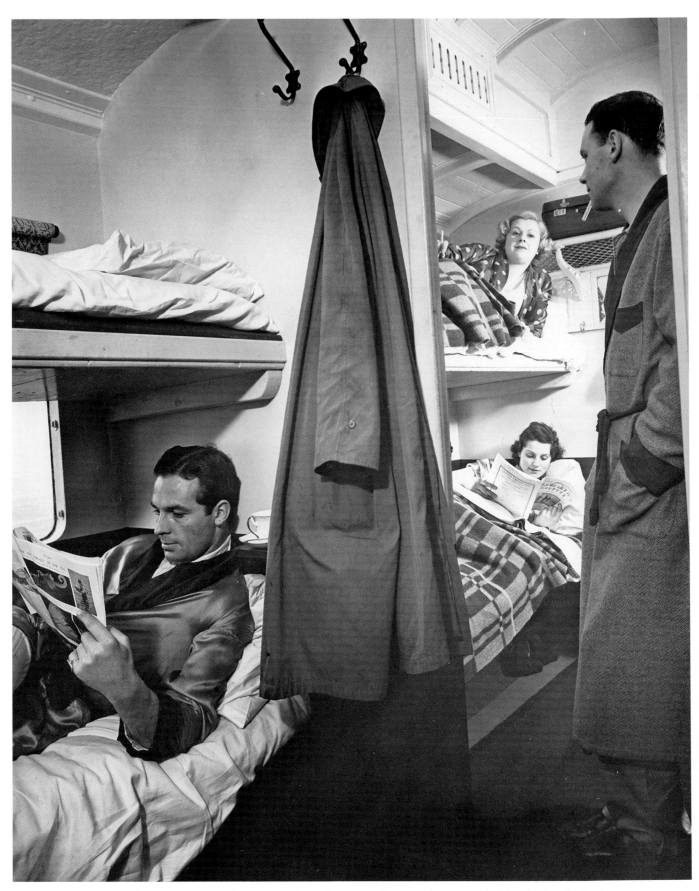

Sleeping accommodation was a bit rudimentary, but people were probably a bit hardier in those days.

GWR AIR SERVICES

The Great Western formed its own Air Service in 1933, initially operated between Cardiff Municipal Airport and Plymouth, and between Birmingham and Liverpool. The first year of operation was not as successful as was hoped, actually producing a net loss. So in March 1934, the Great Western service amalgamated with the other four major railway companies to form Railway Air Services Ltd. This new company was operated in collaboration with Imperial Airways. In this guise, the new air service was much more successful, moving mail, perishable goods, other freight and even livestock. However, many of the services were suspended during the Second World War, and in 1945 and with a new Government, railway involvement in Air Transport ceased.

Brochure advertising the new air service.

A Westland Wessex pictured here at Cardiff Airport on 11 April 1933 ready for the special VIP inaugural flight to Plymouth calling at Exeter en route. The aircraft was flown by Captain Gordon Olley and with five company officials and a newspaper reporter as passengers, it reached Exeter in just 44 minutes. The regular passenger service between Cardiff and Plymouth was introduced on the following day.

Another picture of a Westland Wessex taken again in 1933 at the Midland Aero Club, which at this time was situated at Castle Bromwich. Services to and from this airport had been introduced on 22 May 1933. The Hercules Bicycle Company van is from the nearby factory at Nechells. The two members of staff are apparently loading two Hercules bicycles 'the best that money can buy' onto the aircraft.

A Railway Air Services de Havilland D H 84 Dragon at Cardiff Municipal Airport in May 1934. The two gentlemen in white coats are carrying boxes of Richmond's Sausages, at this time produced in Liverpool.

PASSENGER SHIPPING SERVICES

The Great Western operated a number of shipping services with important routes to the Channel Islands and to Southern Ireland. As early as 1864, the GWR had obtained an Act to allow it to operate steam passenger vessels from New Milford to Waterford and Cork and between Weymouth and the Channel Islands. The New Milford service was taken over on 1 February 1872 from a company run by Captain Jackson of Milford. It operated these services until the opening of the Fishguard Harbour branch on 30 August 1906, after which the services to and from Southern Ireland switched from New Milford (later Neyland) to

Members of office staff and boat crews from the Channel Islands service pose for the photographer outside the GWR offices at Weymouth Quay in January 1901. The boat crews have GWR on their caps, notice also the tramway tracks laid in the set stones.

A great shot of a Channel Islands boat train preparing to depart from Weymouth around the turn of the last century. It is hauled by 0-6-0 no 1376. Built as no 114 for the Bristol and Exeter Railway in September 1874, it was absorbed by the Great Western and renumbered 1876 on 1 January 1876. It operated on the Weymouth tramway from 1886 until 1927. The steamer in view is the *Roebuck* from Milford Haven; it was built in 1897 and was taken into war service in 1914, but was unfortunately sunk at Scapa Flow on 13 January 1915 having slipped its mooring and collided with another ship. Notice also how the lamp is attached to the outside end of the first carriage.

A view of Weymouth Quay in August 1929. Standing in the platform is the recently arrived Channel Islands boat train, which has been split into two portions. The passengers are awaiting the arrival of the *St Julien*. The short platform here required the use of steps for passenger access to and from the train.

A lull in services sees two of the Channel Island ships moored at Weymouth again in August 1929. Nearest the camera is the *Great Western*, built in 1902 by Laird Brothers Birkenhead for the Milford to Waterford service, although as seen here it also operated on the Channel Island services. In 1933 she was renamed *GWR 20* and was scrapped in 1934. The second ship is the *St Julian*; she was built by John Brown for the Channel Islands services in 1925, and used as a hospital ship during the Second World War, taking part in both the Dunkirk evacuation and later the Normandy landings. In 1946, she returned to the Channel Island services and was withdrawn in 1961.

Fishguard. To operate the new service in 1906, three new steamers were constructed; the *St George, St David* and *St Patrick*, a fourth the *St Andrew* was added to the fleet in 1908. The new ships were able to complete the journey in about 3 hours.

In August 1889, the Great Western took over the Weymouth to the Channel Islands steamer service from the Weymouth and Channel Islands Steam Packet Company. To operate the service, the Great Western purchased three new steel built twin screw ships, the *Lynx, Antelope* and *Gazelle* from Laird Brothers of Birkenhead. In 1891, a fourth and slightly larger ship, the *Ibex* was added to the fleet.

Great Western Railway services from Fishguard Harbour to Southern Ireland were inaugurated on 30 August 1906.

GREAT WESTERN RAILWAY.
The Direct Route to IRELAND via FISHGUARD

TO BE OPENED IN SUMMER 1906.

Magnificently appointed
TURBINE STEAMERS, 22½ Knots.
Sea Passage under 3 Hours.

PADDINGTON STATION, W.   JAMES C. INGLIS, GEN. MANAGER.

A postcard advertising the new service to Ireland from Fishguard to Rosslare by the artist Frederick Simpson. The ship illustrated is the *St Patrick* which was one of four similar ships built for this service between 1906 and 1910, the others being the *St Andrew, St David* and *St George*. Unfortunately, the *St Patrick* caught fire at Fishguard in 1929 and was subsequently scrapped.

A great shot of Bulldog no 3381 *Maine* departing from Fishguard Harbour on 2 May 1908 with an up 'Ocean' express service to Paddington.

Arrival of the Mauritania

From August 1909, some of the larger ocean liners started to call at Fishguard en- route from New York to Southampton. By calling here, passengers could travel by special boat trains reaching Paddington in around 5 hours, saving over a day on the sea journey to Southampton. A view of the *Mauritania* moored in Fishguard Bay on 30 August 1909 after its arrival from New York.

Standing on the dock side waiting to greet passengers are a number of suitably attired Welsh girls and members of the dock staff. 30 August 1909.

Also pictured here on 30 August 1909 is the passenger tender vessel *Sir Francis Drake* unloading passengers who have arrived from America. *Sir Francis Drake* was built by Cammell Laird, Birkenhead in 1908. She occasionally operated as a tender at Fishguard, but was mainly used by the Great Western at Plymouth as a tender vessel for some 46 years, being withdrawn from service in 1954.

"Mauretania Special" Fishguard Station.

An official postcard view of 4-4-0s no 3402 Halifax and no 4108 *Hotspur* on a *Mauritania* special to Paddington at Fishguard Harbour on 30 August 1909.

DINING GREAT WESTERN STYLE

ining or Restaurant cars were first introduced by the Great Western in March 1886, initially for first class passengers only and on just two services between Paddington and Bristol and Paddington to Cardiff. In January 1903, the service was extended to many other main line services running to and from Paddington, and for the first time it included all three classes of travel. The food and service provided was said to be second to none.

Postcard facsimile of a poster advertising the extension of Dining Car services across the system. c 1903.

The opulent interior of coach no.405, a 70ft 1st Class 'Concertina' dining coach of 1906/7. This really was dining at its best.

A posed picture taken inside Restaurant Car no 9672 showing passengers being served by an immaculately turned out dining car attendant no 36. circa1935.

Great Western Railway

"KING GEORGE V"—BRITAIN'S MOST POWERFUL PASSENGER LOCOMOTIVE—G.W.R.

Torquay Car (2)	*MENU*	September 22nd, 1927.

3/- LUNCHEON	2/6 LUNCHEON
Roast Mutton & Onion Sauce Curried Beef, Madras Cold Roast Lamb and Mint Sauce Cold Ox Tongue Vegetables and Potatoes	Roast Mutton & Onion Sauce Curried Beef, Madras Cold Roast Lamb and Mint Sauce Cold Ox Tongue Vegetables and Potatoes
Pears Cardinal Cabinet Pudding Fruit Jelly	CHOICE OF Pears Cardinal Cabinet Pudding Fruit Jelly OR
Cheese and Salad Biscuits (Huntley & Palmers)	Cheese and Salad Biscuits (Huntley & Palmers)

Liqueur Coffee, per cup, 4d. extra.

COMPTON CERTIFIED MILK SUPPLIED ON THIS CAR

It is particularly requested that a bill be obtained from the Conductor for all payments.

Communications respecting Restaurant Car Services should be addressed to the Manager of the Hotels, Refreshment Rooms and Restaurant Cars Department, Paddington Station, London, W.2.

Hotels under the Management of the Great Western Railway,

GREAT WESTERN ROYAL HOTEL	-	Paddington, W.2.
TREGENNA CASTLE HOTEL	- -	St. Ives, Cornwall.
FISHGUARD BAY HOTEL	- -	Goodwick, Pembrokeshire.

N.B.—The Cream used on this Restaurant Car is Preserved, containing Boric Acid not exceeding 0.5 per cent
WAVERLEY CIGARETTES served on this Car, 20 for 1/-
The G.W.R. Time Table and " Holiday Haunts " may be referred to on this Car.

THIS MENU MAY BE TAKEN AWAY BY THE PASSENGER

Luncheon Menu for restaurant car 2 on the down Torquay service 27 September 1927. Interestingly on the menu is curried beef Madras, popular today but perhaps a surprising addition on a 1927 Great Western restaurant car menu, although perhaps not as at this time many of the passengers may have served with the Army in India. Also advertised are Waverley cigarettes and Compton certified milk – this was milk that had been certified free from tuberculosis.

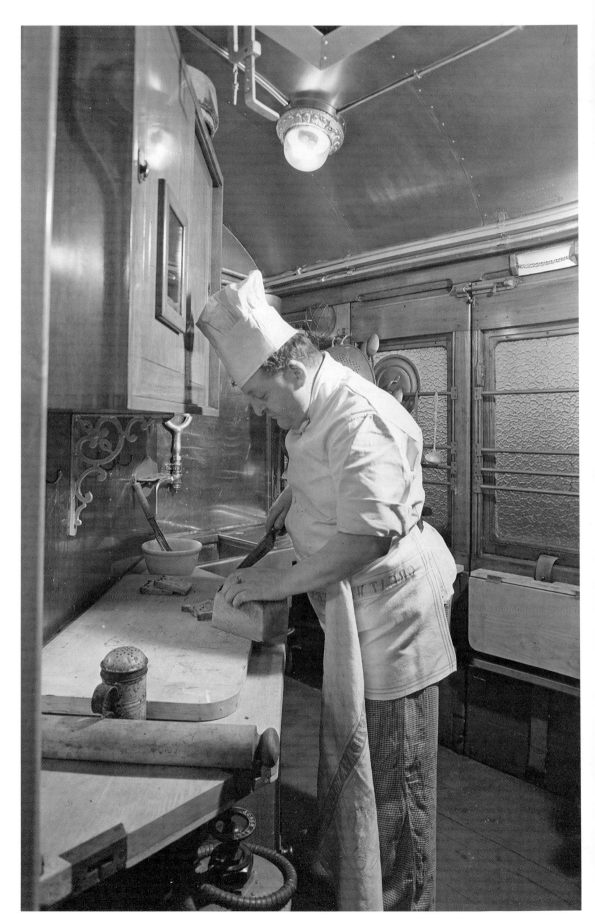

Great Western chef preparing a meal, close examination shows that he is cutting a meat loaf.

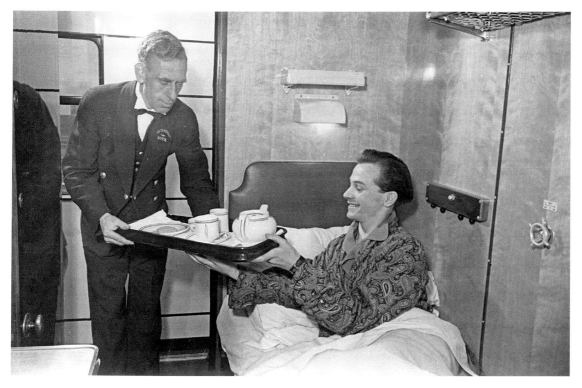

Early morning tea sir? Dining car attendant no 107a serves a delighted traveller in 1st Class sleeping car no 9066 in November 1946.

The interior of one of the twelve wheel buffet cars that were constructed by the Great Western in 1938. The counter had eight chromium plated high stools, with table seating for a further twenty. The couple in the foreground are drinking ginger ale and eating Huntley and Palmers biscuits.

A publicity shot showing Christmas celebrations in the buffet car and the period between the 1st and 2nd world wars probably saw the Great Western at its best.

BRIDGES AND VIADUCTS

Brunel was responsible for the design of many of the bridges and viaducts on the Great Western Railway. Although over the years many of these structures have been altered or replaced, the following images show some in their original condition.

The brick bridge over the Thames at Maidenhead, pictured here in 1893 and shortly after widening. Built to carry two broad gauge lines, it was opened for traffic on 1 July 1839. The bridge comprised two brick arches each 128ft in length, and with a rise of only 24ft the arches are the widest and flattest in the world. The bridge was widened to four tracks and opened for traffic on 4 June 1893, the new section being built in exactly the same style as the original structure.

Brunel's Bridge over the River Wye at Chepstow in around 1890. The bridge was partially opened for traffic with a single track on 19 June 1852, and fully opened with double tracks on 18 April 1853. The main supporting chains of the bridge were carried in the two cast iron cylinders. In 1962, the bridge was extensively rebuilt with modern steel trusses replacing the original cast-iron tubular structure.

Brunel's masterpiece has to be the Royal Albert Bridge which crosses the Tamar River west of Plymouth. This view shows the bridge, taken from Saltash and probably soon after completion. The bridge comprises two 455ft lenticular iron trusses that stand 100ft above the Tamar River. The navy insisted that the bridge should be 100ft above the waterline to allow their sailing ships to pass and Brunel duly obliged. On either side are the approach spans, constructed of plate girders supported on stone piers, the total length of the whole structure being some 2,187 ft. The bridge was opened by Prince Albert on 2 May 1859. Notice the disc and crossbar signal on the west side of the bridge.

Ivybridge station and viaduct beyond, seen here in broad gauge days. This South Devon Railway station was constructed with staggered up and down platforms and was opened on 15 June 1848, and as can be seen was situated to the west of the single line viaduct. This viaduct was constructed of wood supported on stone pillars. It was rebuilt in stone and brick as a two track viaduct in 1893, but was not fully opened for traffic until 1894. Notice the broad gauge gangers trolley dismantled for storage, but ready for assembly and use. The station seen here was closed to passengers in 1959, but a new station at Ivybridge was opened to the east of the viaduct on 15 July 1994.

A broad gauge goods train is seen here crossing the single track wooden Carvedras Viaduct at Truro. One of the many Brunel-designed timber viaducts, it was built by the Cornwall Railway, being opened in May 1859. The wooden structure was replaced in August 1902 with a new double track viaduct constructed of stone.

PADDINGTON

The first station opened at Paddington was a temporary wooden structure that was situated to the west of the Bishops Road Bridge. Constructed for the opening of the railway in 1838, it was closed in 1854 when a new station was opened to the east of the Bishop's Road Bridge. Designed by Brunel and the architect Sir Matthew Digby Wyatt, Paddington was fully opened for traffic on 29 May 1854. The station area was covered by three separate glazed roof sections. Initially there were three arrival and three departure platforms, but over the years the station was improved and altered. The end of the broad gauge in 1892 allowed the number of platforms to be increased to nine. In 1909, work was started to provide three additional platforms, nos 10,11,and 12 at the Bishops Road side of the station. This entailed major engineering work and the addition of a fourth overall roof section, the work being completed in 1916. Further work took place in 1933 when the old Bishop's Road station was demolished and replaced by a new station with four platforms. Opened on 18 September 1933, it was designated Paddington Suburban, its platforms being numbered 13, 14, 15 and 16. At this time, platforms 13 and 16 were served by Hammersmith and City electric services.

An amusing turn of the last century postcard illustrating the 'Cornishman' service at Paddington. The artist has also included the station collecting dog.

raed Street and Paddington Station, London.

A colour postcard of Praed Street, showing Paddington station and the Great Western Hotel. The Hotel was designed by Brunel and Philip Charles Hardwick and was opened on 9 June 1854.In recent years it has had an extensive makeover and is today one of the top London Hotels.

A view looking down at Platform 1 showing to good effect the design of the roof and also the globe lights – an early type of electric lighting installed at Paddington in 1886. The famous three-sided clock was installed in 1903, and can be seen on the right.

3001 class 4-2-2 no 3007 Dragon departs from platform 2 with the 10.15am fast service to Weston-Super-Mare and Minehead in June 1908. In view behind the locomotive is Paddington Departure Signal Box, opened in 1879, constructed of timber it contained a 66-lever frame. In 1933, the box was rebuilt and enlarged to house a 96 lever frame. Opening on 2 July 1933, it remained in use until it was closed on 15 October 1967.

A commercial postcard issued by Wyman's in 1918 with an interesting view of the crowds on platforms 1 and 2 awaiting arrival of empty coaching stock.

An interesting picture of Bulldog 4-4-0 no 3426 *Walter Long* standing at platform 9 and taken around 1900. Notice the horse drawn cabs on the station cab road, and the large retaining wall seen here covered in advertising signs. Parts of this wall, which were 10ft thick, were partially removed during the reconstruction work for the 4th roof.

A typical scene at Paddington. This posed shot was taken on platform 1 in 1935 and shows a group of 'passengers' alongside King no 6007 *King William III*. The time on the clock is 10.25 am which indicates that this is the down 'Cornish Riviera' service, the 10.30 Ltd. Notice also the different design of inside valve covers on the adjacent King.

Paddington was not all about passengers, the station also handled a considerable amount of mail and parcels. Although not of the best quality I have included this picture taken in December 1908 entitled 'Christmas Parcels' which are seen here piled up on platform no.8.

COUNTRY STATIONS

There were hundreds of country stations on the Great Western system, some large, some small. With the extensive closure of branch lines over the years, many of these stations are but a memory, however some of the buildings survive as private dwellings though others have gone forever. I hope that the following pictures will illustrate the heritage that has been lost, and some that has been saved.

Over the years, many postcards were produced illustrating local stations and branch lines. This humorous card from around 1914 draws attention to the slow journey times on the Cholsey to Wallingford branch. I am sure the same sentiments applied to many a Great Western branch line.

A service from Wycombe to Paddington via Maidenhead arriving at Bourne End hauled by an unidentified Queen Class 2-2-2 probably around the 1880s. Bourne End was opened by the Wycombe Railway as Marlow Road on 1 August 1854, it became a junction with the opening of the Marlow branch by the Great Marlow Railway on 28 June 1873, on 1 January 1874 Marlow Road was renamed Bourne End. The Marlow Railway was taken over by the GWR on 6 August 1897 and the on 14 February 1899 the terminus at Great Marlow was renamed Marlow.

The station at Malmesbury in around 1921. The branch from Dauntsey was opened on 18 December 1877. The station and line was closed to passengers on 10 September 1951. In the siding on the right is the Malmesbury station gas supply; this would have been delivered from the gas works at Swindon.

Metro class 2-4-0T no 5 stands at Chard in March 1928. The branch from Creech Junction to Chard
was opened on 11 September 1866. Passengers services from Chard to Taunton were withdrawn on
10 September 1962, but the station remained open for services to Chard Junction until 7 March 1966.

Drybrook Road station pictured here in the early 1920s. The station stood on Cinderford to Coleford line
and opened in 1875. It was closed to passengers on 8 July 1929, however the line remained open for goods
traffic until October 1949. The short freight appears to be hauled by an 1854 class 0-6-0PT.

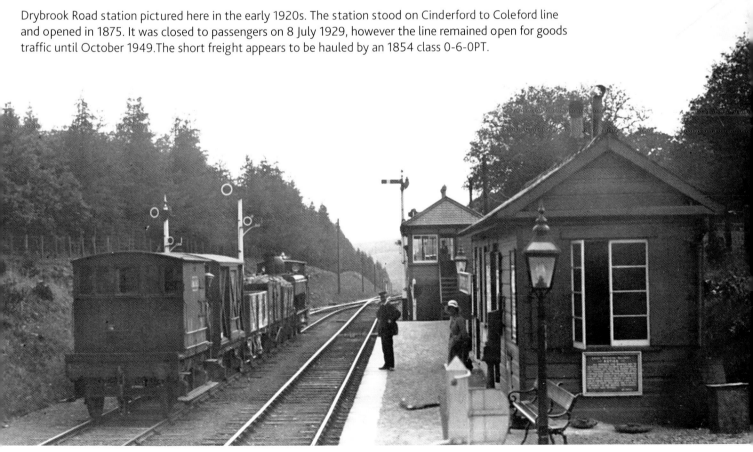

Avonwick was an intermediate station on the Brent to Kingsbridge branch. Here Metro 2-4-0T no 1448 prepares to depart with a service to Kingsbridge in the 1920s. Avonwick closed when passenger services were withdrawn from the Kingsbridge branch on 10 September 1963.

The Uffington to Faringdon branch was opened by the Faringdon Railway Company on 1 June 1854. The terminus station comprised a single platform. The stone station building with attractive twin hipped roofs housed the ticket office and waiting room. It is seen here in 1919 after the arrival of the branch service from Uffington. The stone building on the right is the locomotive shed. The branch closed to passengers on 31 December 1951 and to goods on 1 July 1963. The station building is now listed and stands in the centre of a small industrial estate.

The terminus station at Abbotsbury with the station staff, loco crew and in the foreground, the family of station master Henry Weston. The stone station building was designed by William Clarke. Standing in the platform is a 517 class 0-4-2T with auto-coach no 97. The branch from Upwey Junction was opened on 9 November 1895 and closed to passengers on 1 December 1952.

Blagdon station was the terminus of the Wrington Vale Light Railway and was opened on 4 December 1901. It is seen here on 22 May 1929 with 517 class 0-4-2T no 540 with the 7.20pm branch service to Yatton. The Blagdon branch was closed to passenger traffic on14 September 1931 and to goods on 1 November 1950.

A view of Hemyock on the Culm Valley light railway taken on 8 May 1929 with 2-4-0T no 1300 waiting to depart with the branch service to Tiverton Junction. The branch was opened on 29 May 1876 and was closed to passengers on 7 September 1963, remaining open for milk traffic until 1975. No 1300 was built as a standard gauge side tank in 1878 and was rebuilt at Swindon in February 1905, before being withdrawn in May 1934.

A view of the station at Heathfield in around 1906. A 4500 class 2-6-2T waits at the platform with a branch service. The station was opened as Chudleigh Road by the Moretonhampstead and South Devon Railway on 1 July 1874 and was renamed Heathfield with the opening of the Teign Valley Railway In October 1882. It was closed to passengers on 28 February 1959. The large building on the left is the Candy and Co Pottery, now closed and demolished.

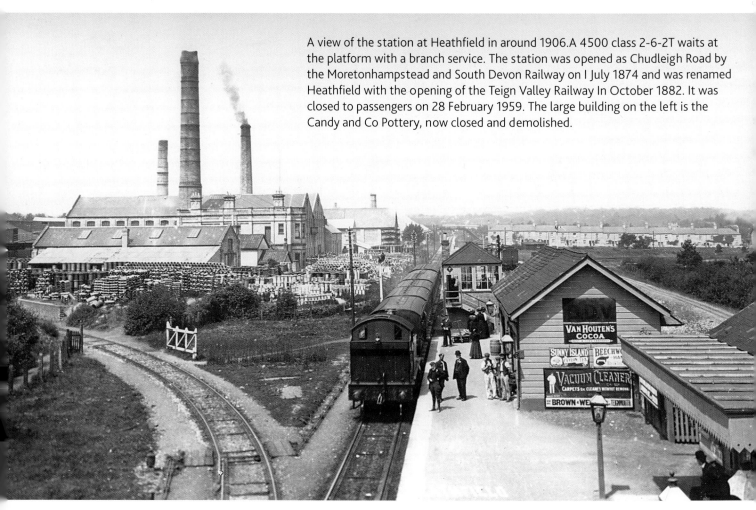

The small terminus station at Newcastle Emlyn with a 4800 class 0-4-2T waiting on the branch with a service to Pencader. The branch was opened by the Great Western on 1 July 1895 and closed to passengers on 15 September 1952. The branch remained open for goods traffic serving the local creamery until 22 September 1973

A high level view of Lifton taken from the Tinhay Tramway Bridge. The station stood on the Launceston branch and was opened on 1 June 1865. In the background is the Ambrosia creamery that was opened in 1917, famous for its rice puddings. The station closed to passengers on 31 December 1962, but the line remained open to serve the creamery siding until 28 February 1966.

2021 class 0-6-0PT no 2055 arrives at Watlington with a service from Princes Risborough on 17 June 1939. The branch was opened by Watlington and Princes Risborough Railway on 15 August 1872, being sold to the GWR in 1883. The line was closed to passengers and goods on 1 July 1957. Part of the branch is now operated by the Chinnor and Princes Risborough Railway.

The stone station at Kerne Bridge with a 517 class 0-4-2T departing with a branch train. The station was opened by the Ross and Monmouth Railway in August 1873 and closed to passengers on 5 January 1959. The building was not demolished and after some years as an activity centre it is currently in use as a private house.

KERNE BRIDGE STATION
NR ROSS

4400 class 2-6-2T No 4403 is seen here shunting at Princetown. The 10¼ mile branch from Yelverton was opened by the GWR on 11 August 1883 and closed to passengers and goods on 5 March 1956.

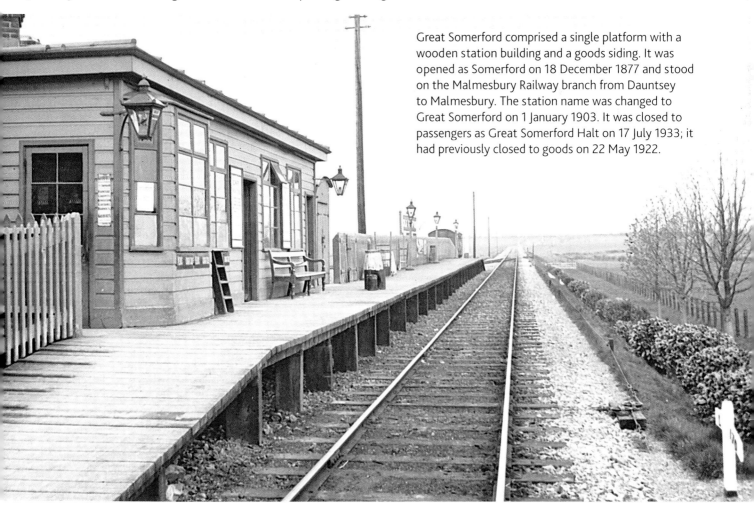

Great Somerford comprised a single platform with a wooden station building and a goods siding. It was opened as Somerford on 18 December 1877 and stood on the Malmesbury Railway branch from Dauntsey to Malmesbury. The station name was changed to Great Somerford on 1 January 1903. It was closed to passengers as Great Somerford Halt on 17 July 1933; it had previously closed to goods on 22 May 1922.

The station at Culham in 1919, Culham was opened as Abingdon Road on 12 June 1844, it was renamed Culham with the opening of the Abingdon branch on 2 June 1856. The station is still open but a new platform has been built on the upside. The original up platform is now closed to the public, the Brunel designed stone station building is listed and is currently in private use.

ROYAL TRAINS

The close proximity of the Great Western main line and the opening of the Slough to Windsor branch on 8 October 1849 ensured that the Great Western had a long association with royalty. Prince Albert had first travelled on the Great Western between Slough and Paddington on 14 November 1839 but it was to be another three years before Queen Victoria travelled on the railway. In anticipation of this event the Great Western constructed a Royal Saloon in July 1840. The Queen's first trip using the new saloon was made between Slough and Paddington on Monday 13 June 1842, the train which was hauled by the broad gauge engine Phlegathon was driven by Daniel Gooch. Queen Victoria was the first British Monarch to travel by train; and from this first journey every British Monarch since has used the convenience of the train to travel to their many official engagements throughout the country.

The interior of the Queen's saloon ,built at Swindon for Queen Victoria's diamond jubilee in 1897. It was one of six new coaches built at Swindon at this time for the new royal train. The coach is now preserved at the Steam Museum Swindon.

An official photograph of the royal train at Swindon around the turn of the last century. The locomotive is the Gooch single no.3041 The Queen, the royal saloon is the fourth vehicle in the formation.

The Queen passed away at Osbourne House on 22 January 1901 and the Great Western were asked to provide a funeral train from Paddington to Windsor on Saturday 2 February 1901.

The funeral train was hauled by Atbara class 4-4-0 no 3373 Atbara , which was temporarily renamed Royal Sovereign for the occasion. It is pictured here at Old Oak Common suitably decorated with a smokebox wreath and the Royal Coat of Arms.

An official card produced for the funeral train showing the formation and seating details. The funeral was attended by what was probably the largest number of European royalty ever assembled in one place.

GREAT · WESTERN · RAILWAY.
FUNERAL OF
Her Late Most Gracious Majesty The Queen.
ARRANGEMENT OF ROYAL TRAIN.
Paddington to Windsor 1·32 p.m. Saturday 2nd Feby 1901.

ENGINE.	BRAKE VAN.	SEMI-SALOON.	COMPARTMENTS.	SALOON.	SALOON.	ROYAL SALOON.	SALOON.	SALOON.	SALOON.	SEMI-SALOON.	COMPARTMENTS.	BRAKE VAN.
ROYAL SOVEREIGN.	Guard. T. King.	ROYAL FOOTMEN AND ATTENDANTS.	Mr A Hubbard.	Lt Col Sir A. Bigge.	Col. H.H. Mathias.	Duke of Portland. Duke of Norfolk.	H.M. THE KING. H.M. THE QUEEN.	H.R.H. Duke of Cambridge.	Duc D'Alencon.	Non-Com Officers and Men of German Army Deputation.	Earl Cawdor.	Guar... W.J. fow...
Mr J Armstrong.	Mr W.H. Weister.		Mr Robinson.	Lt Col R.Ith Sir F.I. Edwards.	Col. W. Aitken.	COFFIN OF HER LATE MOST GRACIOUS MAJESTY.	H.R.H. Duke of Connaught. H.R.H. Ds. of Fife.	H.M. King of the Hellenes. H.H. Prince Ch. of Saxe Weimar.	Ds. of Buccleuch. Countess of Lytton.		Mr J.L. Wilkinson.	Interpr... Lieu...
Insp W.Greenaway.	Mr E. Rendell.		Mr T.I. Allen.	Col. J. Brocklehurst.	Col. E.T. Hutton.	Earl of Clarendon. Earl of Pembroke.	H.I.M. The Kaiser. H.R.H. Ps. Victoria.	H.M. King of the Belgians. H.R.H. D. of Boden.	Miss Phipps. Lady Suffield. Miss Knollys.			Ham...
Driver: D. Hughes.			Mr W.A. Hart.	Lt. Col. The Hon W.P. Carrington.	Capt. Sir E. Chichester.		H.R.H. Duke of Saxe Coburg. H.R.H. Charles of Denmark.	H.M. King of Portugal. H.R.H.P. Arnulf of Bavaria.				Mess "N" Wilso...
Fireman G. Bayliss.				Lt. Col. A. Davidson.	Capt. E.S. Poë.		Crown Prince of Germany. H.R.H. Ps. Christian.	H.R.H. Prince Christian. H.R.H. D. of Wurtemberg.				R.M...
				Lt. Col. Hon. H.C. Legge.	Capt. Count F.C. Metaxa.		Prince Arthur of Connaught. H.R.H. Ds. of Argyll.	H.R.H. G.D. of Hesse. H.R.H. P. of Waldeck Permanst.				Grego...
				Capt. F. Ponsonby.	Capt. W.H. May.		Prince Henry of Prussia. H.R.H. P. of Battenberg.	H.R.H. D. of Sparta. H.S.H Hereditary P. Hohenlohe-Langenburg.				F. Hylar...
				Sir J. Reid.	Col. B.G.D. Cooke.		Crown Prince of Denmark. H.H. Ds. of Saxe Coburg.	H.R.H.C.P of Norway & Sweden. H.R.H.P of Hohenzollern.				A. Bau...
				Lord Suffield.	Col. Lord Blythswood.		Prince Charles of Denmark. H.R.H. Ds. of Connaught.	Crown Prince of Roumania. H.R.H.P Philip of Saxe Coburg.				T. P...
				Lord Lawrence.	Col. J.H. Rivett-Carnac.		H.R.H. Ds. of Albany. H.R.H. Ps. Adolph of Schaumberg-Lippe.	H.R.H Archduke of Austria. H.H. D of Mecklenburg Strelitz.				Llewe...
				Lord Churchill.	Col. J. Stevenson.			H.R.H. D. of Aosta. H.R.H Hereditary P. of Saxe Meiningen.				L.W...
				Lord Colville of Culross.	Col. Earl of Harewood.			H.H. D. of Ernest Gunther. H.R.H.C. P. of Siam.				Mead...
				Col. Brabazon.	Col. Duke of Beaufort.			H.H.P.F.C of Hesse. H.S.H.P. Francis of Teck.				
				Col. H. Ricardo.	Col. C.B. Bashford.			H.S.H. D.G. of Teck. Prince Henry of Reuss.				
				Capt. Holford.	Col. Earl of March.			H.H.P. Leopold of Saxe Coburg. Duke of Fife.				
				Col. J.C. Cavendish.	Col. Duke of Montrose.			H.H.P Mohammed Ali Pacha. H.R.H. D. of Saxony.				
				Col. Sir R. Ogilvy.	Brevet-Col. T.F.D. Bridge.			H.S.H.P Ernest of Saxe-Altenburg. H.S.H.P. Adolph of Schaumberg-Lippe.				
				Col. Duke of Northumberland.	Col. H.N. Mc.Rae.			H.H.P Albert of Schleswig Holstein. H.S.H Pof Hohenlohe Langenburg.				
				Col. Marquis of Londonderry.	Col. H.G. Dixon.			H.S.H.P Alexander of Teck.				
				Col. Earl of Haddington.	Col. G.L.C. Money.							
				Col. Viscount Galway.	Capt. Hon H. Lambton.							
				Col. C.P. Le Cornu.	Capt. C. Campbell.							
				Col. J. Davis.	Capt. A. Mac Leod.							
				Col. W. Martin.	Capt. A.A.C. Parr.							
				Col. W. Bell.	Capt. G.L. Atkinson.							
				Col. W. Campbell.								

T.I. ALLEN, Supt of the Line

EARL CAWDOR, Chairman.
G.K. MILLS, Secretary.

J.L. WILKINSON, Gen. Mar...

Queen Victoria was succeeded by King Edward V11, this photograph shows the royal train passing Brent on 7 March 1902 hauled by Bulldog Class 4-4-0 no 3345 which also had been temporarily named Royal Sovereign. The train is conveying King Edward V11 and Queen Alexandra to Dartmouth (via Kingswear). On arrival at Dartmouth the King laid the foundation stone for the new Royal Naval College.

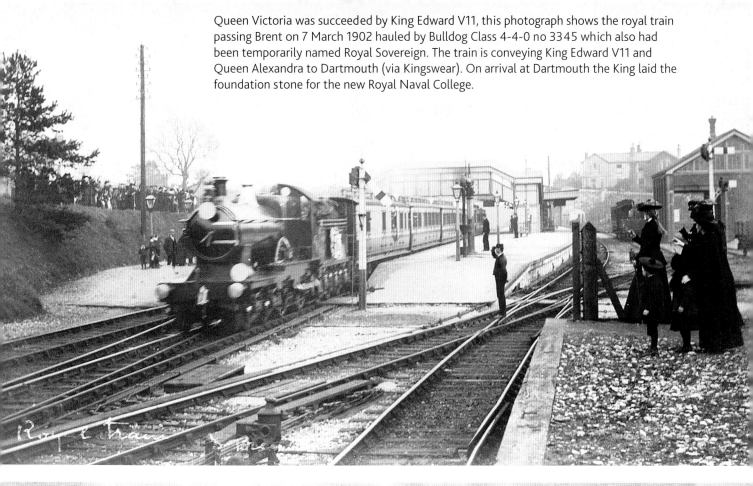

Another postcard showing the royal train at Gloucester on 23 June 1909 hauled by Star Class 4-6-0 no 4021 Kind Edward. The King was on an official visit to what was reported as a rather muddy Royal Agricultural show at Gloucester.

Edward V11 died on 6 May 1910 being succeeded by King George V. The new king together with Queen Mary are seen here after arriving at Treherbert on 27 June 1912. The King and Queen were on a three day visit to South Wales , on the previous day the King had laid the foundation stone of the National Museum of Wales. They also visited the Lewis Merthyr Colliery at Trehafod and the Mines Rescue centre at Dinas.

The royal funeral train, hauled by Castle Class no 4082 Windsor Castle carrying the late King George V en-route from Paddington to Windsor , is seen here passing Langley on 29 January 1936. The King had died at Sandringham on 20 January 1936. On an official visit to Swindon works on 28 April 1924 the King had driven the newly constructed no 4082 from the works to the station, so it was fitting that this locomotive should be used to haul his funeral train.